IT HAPPENS

TRUE TALES FROM THE TRENCHES OF YOUTH MINISTRY

WILL PENNER, GENERAL EDITOR

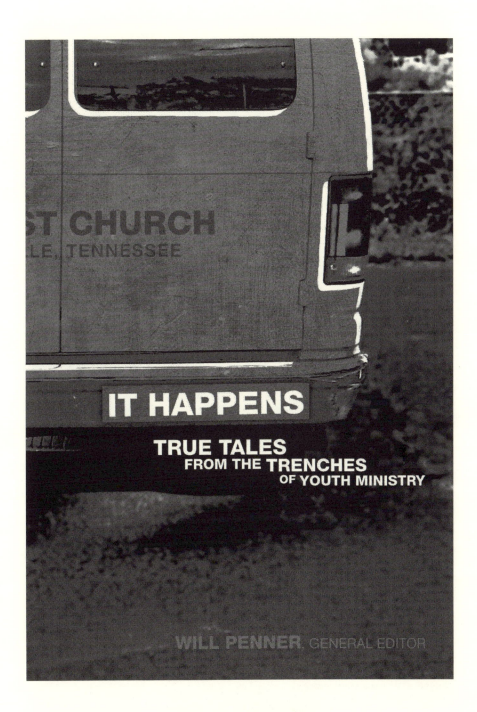

⊙cymt

CYMT Press

It Happens
©2012 by Will Penner

CYMT Press is an imprint of the Center for Youth Ministry Training; 309 Franklin Road, Brentwood, Tennessee 37027.

ISBN 978-1-937734-04-6

Unless otherwise indicated, all Scripture quotations are taken from the New Revised Standard Version of the Bible, ©1989 by the Division of Christian Education of the National Council of Churches of the United States of America.

All rights reserved. No part of this publication may be reproduced, stored in a retrieval system, or transmitted in any form or by any means--electronic, mechanical, photocopy, recording, or any other--(except for brief quotations in printed reviews) without the prior permission of the publisher.

Web site addresses listed in this book were current at the time of publication. Please contact Center for Youth Ministry Training via e-mail (Info@CYMT.org) to report URLs that are no longer operational and replacement URLs if available.

Editorial direction by Mindi Godfrey
Art direction by David Conn

Printed in the United States

TABLE OF CONTENTS

1. **Introduction:** Getting the Most out of This Book   9
Will Penner

SECTION 1: DEALING WITH YOUNG PEOPLE

Extra Grace Required

2. **Sexting:** The Kid Whose Dirty Deeds Are Publicly Revealed   17
Bart Campolo

3. **The Inquisitor:** The Kid Who Questions Everything   23
Cory Peacock

4. **Don't Shoot:** The Kid With Severe Mental Health Issues   29
Scott Gillenwaters

5. **Gossip Train:** The Kid Who Feeds on Talking about Others   37
Syler Thomas

6. **The Criminal:** The Kid Facing Charges   45
Susan Groce

Policy Issues

7. **Assertive Yet Inviting:** Discipline at Church   51
Jack Radcliffe

8. **Alcohol:** When Parents Encourage Underage Consumption   57
Hank Hilliard

9. **Beyond Thongs and Midriffs:** Dress Code for the 21st Century   65
Dixon Kinser

10. **The Big Trip Question:** To Send Him Home or Not to Send Him Home?   73
Karen Jones

Programs and Events

11. **It's Under Water:** Youth Talks Gone Wrong   79
Matt Laidlaw

12. **Stranded:** Figuring It Out on the Fly   87
    Amy Jacober

13. **Lesson Derailed:** Gossip about the Leader   93
    Drew Smith

14. **Snowed In:** Severe Weather and Quickly Changing Plans 99
    Oeland Camp

15. **9-1-1:** Youth Trips and Hospital Visits   107
    Kelly Soifer

16. **Mistake Snowball:** When one Bad Decision Leads to Another 115
    Sara Bailey

SECTION 2: DEALING WITH ADULTS

Parents

17. **Disgruntled:** The Anger-Ridden Parent   123
    Jim Hampton

18. **High-Maintenance:** The Helicopter Parent   129
    Steve Argue

19. **Smug:** The Smarter-Than-You Parent   137
    Len Evans

20. **Gone:** Parents Who Vote with Their Feet   143
    Doug Ranck

Volunteers

21. **Boundary Issues:** When Volunteers Date Each Other   151
    Troy Howley

22. **Too Close for Comfort:** Opposite-Gender Relationships 157
    Danette Matty

23. **Crossing the Line:** When Volunteers Date Kids   167
    Mark Montgomery

24. **Crossing Over:** Coming Out of the Closet   175
    Dave Wright

Church Leadership

25. **New Job Responsibilities:** "…and All Other Duties   181
    as Assigned by the Senior Pastor"
    Heather Shaw

26. **My Way or the Highway:** Conflict Resolution at Its Best   189
    and Worst
    Dan Lambert

27. **Witch Hunt:** Parents' Unending Lists of Wrongs   195
    Sally Chambers

28. **Budget Cuts:** The Good, the Bad, and the Necessary   203
    Josh Bishop

29. **Lots of Apologies Necessary:** When We're the ones   211
    Who Screw It Up
    Jay Delp

30. **Married With Children:** When Childbearing   217
    and Job Seeking Collide
    Kenda Dean

31. **Surprise! You're Fired:** Finishing the Race and Ending Well   225
    Brent Parker

INTRODUCTION
GETTING THE MOST
OUT OF THIS BOOK

Will Penner has been working with young people for more than two decades as a youth minister, teacher, coach, and principal. He is a popular speaker for youth events and youth leader trainings, and he is a popular youth ministry consultant. He has written for five publishers, and has served as the editor of *The Journal of Student Ministries and Youthworker Journal.* He lives outside Nashville, Tennessee, with his wife, Christine, and five children ranging in age from 2 to 20. You can contact Will through willpenner.com.

"The best laid plans of mice and men often go awry."

My mom was fond of that old saying. She would use that to try to calm me down when things weren't going my way, though it seldom helped when I was younger. She would also say it to herself from time to time. I didn't understand why; in fact, I always thought it a little odd that she'd talk to herself at all.

These days, I talk to myself all of the time, so I don't think it's nearly as weird as I used to. If myself starts talking back and I learn something I didn't know before, then I'll start to worry.

But now I realize she was simply trying to talk herself into keeping things in perspective when they weren't going the way she had planned. It's a good skill, I think—one that I need to practice more in my own life and ministry.

Unfortunately, while I like to think of myself as incredibly spontaneous, the truth is, I still tend to freak out a little when things don't go like I'd planned. After a couple of decades of working with youth, one might think I'd have learned to overcome the desire for everything to go according to plan. After all, I can't actually remember a single program or event—even a single lesson—that's gone exactly as I had expected.

In conversations with hundreds of other youth workers through the years, I've found that I am not alone in that regard. While we have many different ministry philosophies, styles, traditions, mannerisms, and quirks, we all share at least one common truth: In life, in youth ministry…stuff happens.

IT HAPPENS…

It happens when we least expect it…and when we try to plan for it.

It happens when we are new to youth ministry…and when we've been at it for a long time.

It happens when we're by ourselves…and when the whole world is watching.

It happens when we're spiritually full…and when we're spiritually parched.

It happens where we live and work…and when we're far, far away.

It happens while we're paying attention…and while we're distracted.

It happens because we failed to do something…and despite us doing everything right.

11

It happens for us, against us, by us, around us, beside us, through us, and to us.

If we're out there putting one foot in front of the other, trying our best to serve God through ministry with kids, stuff is going to happen.

And as my dad is fond of saying, "If you don't think God has a sense of humor, try telling him your plans."

SHARING EXPERIENCES

What I've learned though, is that when we share our stories with one another, several amazing things occur.

First, and perhaps most importantly, we recognize that we're not alone. Youth ministry can be a lonely enterprise at times. Colleagues on our church staffs don't understand what we do. Friends from outside church often think we're nuts to want to spend so much time around teenagers. But when we read or hear stories about other youth workers' experiences, often we feel a great sense of relief, realizing we're not alone out there.

Second, we get to see how others have handled tough situations and what they learned from the experiences. Sometimes we learn specific, practical tips that we can apply to a similar program or event in our ministries. Even better, sometimes we can learn some principles that can be generalized to many situations in our ministries, even dissimilar ones.

Third, we are often provided with a mirror to some of our own experiences. We see how our own joys, fears, choices, struggles, hopes, and anxieties are echoed by our colleagues; and sometimes, seeing those experiences articulated by others helps us give voice to experiences of our own from which we can learn and grow.

That's why we put together this book.

EXPERIENTIAL LEARNING

Readers who are familiar with educational psychologist David Kolb's Experiential Learning Model may recognize his four elements throughout the following pages—sometimes explicitly stated, sometimes implicitly suggested. For those not familiar, basically Kolb suggested that adults generally learn best through four stages:

- Concrete experiences
- Reflections on those experiences

- Forming abstract principles based on the reflections
- Testing new theories, leading to new concrete experiences

Our hope is that as you read about all of the stuff that happens in the trenches of youth ministry—the concrete experiences from real youth workers—along with some of the authors' reflections, and in some cases, principle formation—that you'll find yourself reflecting on your own experiences with the text and forming new principles that you can try out in your youth ministry.

We also invite you to share with us your own true tales from the trenches. Write about the stuff that's happened in your ministry and what you learned from it. Send your stories to will@willpenner.com, and we may post your stories online at cymt.org or in a future edition of *It Happens*.

Be blessed as you share in the experiences of your colleagues, gleaning wisdom and insight that you can use in your own youth ministry.

SECTION 1:
DEALING WITH YOUNG PEOPLE

SEXTING
THE KID WHOSE DIRTY DEEDS
ARE PUBLICLY REVEALED

Bart Campolo is a veteran urban minister and activist who speaks and writes about grace, faith, loving relationships and social justice. Bart is the leader of The Walnut Hills Fellowship, a local ministry in inner city Cincinnati. He is also the outreach coordinator of Abraham's Path and executive director of **EAPE**, which develops and supports innovative, cost-effective mission projects around the world.

It was late when Karen came over from next door with her cell phone. On the line was Emily, a young schoolteacher who moved here with her husband to be part of our fellowship, and who has been especially good to Jamilla, an against-the-odds teenager on her block. Karen put Emily on speaker, and suddenly we were all together in the middle of a postmodern teenage nightmare.

With part of her disability check, Jamilla had gotten herself a high-status cell phone that connects with internet, and recently she had been experimenting with 'Urban Chat,' a sleazy local website where teenagers flirt with each other online. A few hours earlier, an attractive guy from that site had convinced her to send him a nude photograph. Now he was telling her that unless she paid him $60, he was going to forward that photo to every kid he knew at her school. According to Emily, Jamilla was frantic, embarrassed, and very much afraid.

The ensuing conversation ranged from the new dangers of technology to the old vulnerabilities of adolescent insecurity to the unique blind spots of kids in poverty, but it kept coming back to the problem at hand: What should Emily tell Jamilla to do?

Jamilla was frantic, embarrassed, and very much afraid.

DILEMMAS

Certainly, avoiding the situation altogether would have been the best course, and we suddenly wished we had organized some pre-emptive discussions with our teenagers about the danger of sending pornographic images to other people, and more generally treating our bodies as temples of the Holy Spirit. But Jamilla had a more pressing question: to pay or not to pay?

On one hand, Jamilla could refuse the demand and call the guy's bluff. Because she knew nothing about him however, that seemed pretty risky to all of us.

On the other hand, she could pay him the $60 with the hope that her blackmailer would keep the photo to himself. Of course, there was no guar-

19

antee that he wouldn't return to threaten her with exposure again and again, taking advantage of her quite justifiable fear.

For good reasons, Jamilla was terrified to tell her highly dysfunctional family, and it didn't take much research on our part to discover she could get into big trouble for sending the photo in the first place. This was a call we had to make ourselves.

MY RESPONSE

In the end we had Emily tell her to agree to pay off her blackmailer the next morning, in person, on the campus of the University of Cincinnati. Of course, we had another plan in mind.

Jamilla and I parked near the meeting place early. She walked there alone, while I stood across the street, pretending to talk on my cell phone. Both of us nervously scanned the face of every young man on the sidewalk, looking for the bad guy. When he finally showed up, he walked towards Jamilla with a confident smile. Before he could say a word though, I stepped between them.

"My name is Bart Campolo, and I'm Jamilla's pastor," I said calmly, as his smile disappeared. "I've spoken with our lawyer and also with a police officer in our fellowship, and both of them tell me you're not in any real trouble yet." I paused for a moment, hoping he wouldn't run; fortunately, he was frozen in place. "Now first of all, I need to watch you delete that photograph from your cell phone." Wordlessly, he complied.

"Of course," I continued, "you might have a copy of that photo on your computer, but I'm here to tell you that if it goes anywhere, I will personally see to it that you go to jail for at least a year and that your family pays out a great deal of money. Do you understand me?"

He nodded, as I held up my camera and pushed the button. "Now I have your photograph and your telephone number, and I know where you go to school. Son, what you did to Jamilla was ugly and cruel, but I'm going to let you walk away from it. But I promise you, if we ever hear from you again, the wrath of God will come down on you. Again, do you understand me?"

He looked me in the eye for the first time. "Yes sir," he said.

I stepped back. "All right then. You may go."

As he walked away, I put my arm around Jamilla, who still looked very afraid. Honestly, I was a little bit weak in the knees myself. I'm not a natural tough guy, after all.

"Do you really think it's over?" she asked quietly.

"Yes, I do," I replied. "That boy is terrified, and he ought to be. Do you know why?"

"No."

"Because I wasn't bluffing. I meant every word I said."

"Really?"

"Really."

On our way to her high school, I gave Jamilla just the kind of fatherly talking to you would expect, about trust and men and self-respect, and Jamilla gave me just the kind of relieved, grateful attention you would expect after an ordeal like that. Over and over, I tried to communicate to her just how precious she is to us. Jamilla teared up and told me how much it meant to have caring, grown-up friends like Emily in her life. Without Emily, she said, she didn't know where she would be.

After I dropped her off, I called Emily and Karen so they could stop worrying. Then I gave thanks for women like them, who live out their love in the most natural ways—making safe havens for girls in trouble. And then I treated myself to a greasy diner breakfast, during which I reflected at some length on the peculiar exhilaration of utterly overpowering a mean, abusive person in the name of Jesus.

> I reflected at some length on the peculiar exhilaration of utterly overpowering a mean, abusive person in the name of Jesus.

It doesn't happen nearly often enough, but I do love the smell of justice in the morning!

QUESTIONS TO CONSIDER

What are the dangers to responding to this kind of situation this way? What if the guy had responded differently? What if Jamilla's parents found out that her pastor knew about her actions and didn't tell them?

How dirty do our own hands need to get in order to help pull kids out of their messes? How dirty did God's hands get? What are the dangers to us?

What would your boss want you to do in this situation? How about the church board? How would you want a youth leader to act if your son or daughter were in Jamilla's shoes?

THE INQUISITOR
THE KID WHO QUESTIONS EVERYTHING

Cory Peacock currently spends most of his days playing with his two daughters and/or writing his dissertation. He has written for youth ministry magazines, is a volunteer youth leader, and is married to the prettiest professor of youth ministry ever. And he loves baseball (especially the San Francisco Giants), the ukulele, and board games.

There's an old Calvin and Hobbes comic strip, written and drawn by the comic genius Bill Watterson, in which the precocious six-year-old Calvin has a nice father-son talk about things scientific. Calvin asks, "Where does the sun go when it sets?"

Calvin's dad responds, "The sun sets in the West. In Arizona actually. Near Flagstaff."

It's funny because it's true. Wait...no. It's funny because Calvin's dad is playing on that intersection found in younger kids where the depth of their inquisitiveness is matched only by the trust they place in someone, usually their parents. Calvin's credulity is due, in part, to his age, but it is no less due to the relationship he has with his father.

The fact that Calvin believes his dad is evidenced by his facial expressions throughout the strip and the comment he makes to his mother when she puts him to bed for the night. He says, "I hope someday I'm as smart as Dad is."

This poor kid just wants to know where the sun goes when he can't see it and believes the stories his dad tells him about that which he can, at that moment, only take on faith. Calvin's dad means no harm, but he should have known better. If you've ever read the strip, you know that Calvin has an active imagination that needs no fuel for the fire. This, though, is one of the recurring themes of the comic strip. Calvin approaches his dad with sincere questions and is told the most fanciful stories, perhaps because it's fun or perhaps because it's a small way of messing with his own kid's mind as payback for all the questions.

Calvin's dad is actually a good dad, overall. He really wants to build character in his son as is seen in numerous strips, but he just seems unable to deal with Calvin's inquisitiveness in a straightforward way. Calvin's dad is just having fun, but he's missed an opportunity here.

"THAT KID"

It seems that while the inquisitiveness of some kids never abates, the trustfulness does. It seems that way, but it's not entirely true. When I was a teen, there was *that kid* who just asked every question that came to his mind. The filter that was supposed to reside between his brain and mouth was thin—or sometimes nonexistent.

To the uninitiated of that group, and frankly some of the long-term participants of the group, it appeared that this kid didn't trust anything anybody said. If the Sunday school teacher claimed X, he argued for Y. If the youth pastor said Z, he said, but that implies A, B, and C. Seriously, couldn't this kid just trust what they were saying? Why did he have to pick at every answer? Did he think that he was smarter than the leaders? Was he just trying to make trouble? The answers were: he did, genetics, no, and no. How can I be so sure of those answers? I was *that kid*.

I trusted my youth pastor, my senior pastor, the leaders of my Sunday school class, and other leaders. In fact, my trust of those important individuals in my life and my relationships with them were the very reasons I felt I could ask those questions of them. I was told later that several of those leaders did not feel like I trusted them. They really thought at times I was trying to ruin their lesson plans or co-opt the class, but I really wasn't. Okay, once in a while I was; but the majority of the time, it was because they would raise a question or issue that just compelled me to ask a question.

A force greater than myself whispered something in my ear then stood behind me pushing on my back until I spoke up and…*(sigh) there he goes again.* I really wasn't trying to make trouble. I won't lie and say that I didn't appreciate being on the opposite side of what I perceived to be everybody else in the room. Those me-against-the-world type moments were exhilarating, but they were generated by genuine questions. I would not have wanted everyone against me if I had nothing in my six-shooter of questions or answers.

And to answer one more of the questions above: No, I didn't think I was smarter than my leaders. But I did wonder why some of their lessons or answers were so pat and had what I thought were so many obvious holes or exceptions. I really wanted a genuine conversation. I didn't want simple answers boiled down to tasteless gruel.

> I really wanted a genuine conversation. I didn't want simple answers boiled down to tasteless gruel.

The question that I most want to answer here, though, is the one about why I did it. Bart Simpson once said, "I don't know why I did it. I don't know why I enjoyed it. I don't know why I'll do it again." Or something like that.

But I do. For one, I'm inquisitive. Two, I loved to think through the implications of a statement and see how far and which direction those implications would go. But most importantly, I did it because of something my dad said to me. He said, "If God is God, he can stand the questions." That was so freeing. Dad conveyed to me that any question I had, or any answer I came up with, did not change the reality of God. God is God. My little questions and answers do not change that.

GOD CAN TAKE IT

Sometimes, I think we fear that certain questions should be off limits because of what it does to the youth group, the church, or the reality of the world, the heavens, and even God himself—as if God could not handle the questions of some curious teenager. What my dad really did in saying that to me was to free me from the constraints of answers that did not sit well with me theologically so that I might chase down answers that did.

> Sometimes, I think we fear that certain questions should be off limits because of what it does to the youth group, the church, or the reality of the world, the heavens, and even God himself—as if God could not handle the questions of some curious teenager.

That is not to say I had free reign. Don't forget the first part of his quote: "If God is God..." Dad's implication, of course, is that God IS God. So, I couldn't simply develop my own theological understandings based on my own developing ideas. Rather, as an Arminian, I had to think through things theologically by examining the Bible, by consulting my spiritual tradition, by dialoguing with my community of faith, and through prayerful consideration of my life and reason. What my dad hoped for was that the Spirit would draw me to God by means that made sense to me, that spoke to me.

QUESTIONS WELCOME

Since I've "grown up," I've been involved in several youth groups, and each one has *that kid*. Turn about is fair play, eh? As you might imagine, I have a little bit of patience for those kids. I allow them to ask the questions they have as frequently as I can.

I don't let them co-opt the entire time together, because that's not fair to the other young adults who have different interests and questions. But I don't just shut them down. I usually either engage them in that setting or validate their inquisitiveness and ask if we can stay on the particular path we're currently on, but that I'd be happy to pursue this with them later over a hot beverage of their choice.

> It doesn't always work. It's frequently annoying. It certainly takes more time and effort.

It doesn't always work. It's frequently annoying. It certainly takes more time and effort. But I have to remember that the question was raised because there was something in this setting that said to *that kid*, "It's okay to ask your questions here." I want to honor that. Maybe I'll be there as some kid figures out how God IS God when I take the time to engage their questions.

Now, if only I could get my two-year-old daughter to stop asking, "Why?" every four seconds. Does that undermine everything I've just written?

QUESTIONS TO CONSIDER

Does my leadership style insist upon trite, pat answers to deep questions, or do I allow for inquisitiveness among students?

In what ways do I limit young people's understanding of God by inhibiting their questions? What questions, if any, are out of bounds, and why?

How can embracing kids' questions become the norm among all of our youth leaders?

DON'T SHOOT
THE KID WITH SEVERE
MENTAL HEALTH ISSUES

Scott Gillenwaters has been directing youth ministries for more than 25 years. He is the author of *Sage Advice: Stories from Seasoned Youth Workers,* as well as numerous articles and curricula. He enjoys spending time with his wife and two teenage sons (both of whom are in his youth group), and he currently serves First United Methodist Church in Oak Ridge, Tennessee as Director of Student Ministries.

Clay was a small, freckled-faced guy with strawberry blonde hair and an insatiable desire to be liked. He loved to talk to anyone who would listen, and was just as comfortable talking with adults as with his peers. He was a sensitive soul who, as he got older, had a natural rapport with the girls. He was a great listener, and the girls seemed to flock to him. However, although he was friend to many beautiful girls, he was always just a friend.

Long before I ever met them, Clay and his two sisters were adopted by a wealthy family in our church. Although Clay knew his biological family, they were simply unable to afford to take care of him and his sisters. He and his adopted family attended church whenever the doors were open.

As Clay grew into adolescence, his normal teenage angst became a little beyond normal. His ADHD medication was increased, and he saw a counselor regularly. He was always in trouble at school and home, while his two sisters seemed able to do no wrong. His adoptive parents seemed to resent him, and his summers were spent away at various camps—church camp, soccer camp, scout camp, etc. Eventually, he was even sent to a private school during the winter.

My relationship with Clay was a shallow one. I talked with him when he was in town, but because he was so seldom around, getting to know him was difficult. As he felt more and more rejected by his adoptive parents, he became more and more depressed. Conversations I had with him were strained and filled primarily with a regurgitation of his understanding of what his counselors had told him over the years. He talked about all the different medications he was taking and all the conditions and syndromes with which he had been diagnosed.

During his junior year of high school, he returned to our town, our school, and our church. He was playing soccer for the school; and, although he struggled a bit academically, he seemed to be handling life quite well. He struggled with his ADHD medication, often not taking it regularly because he didn't like the way it made him feel. He internalized nearly everything that happened to him. A benign look from someone was interpreted as hatred, an innocent comment construed as a criticism, and normal interactions seen as attacks. To top it off, the girls he liked romantically never seemed to like him back.

DILEMMA

Clay didn't come around the church too often that year, but I had occasion to talk with him now and then. Our relationship deepened as he began to trust me. As spring came, Clay seemed even more troubled. He signed up for our spring retreat and spent a weekend in the mountains with us. Although he spoke a little during the retreat, he seemed distant, choosing not to interact with the other youth even though many efforts were made to include him.

The week after the retreat he called me and asked if he could come by and talk with me, so we set up a time after school the next day. I wasn't sure I could help Clay, but I welcomed the chance to see what was on his mind.

About 10:00 the next morning, I received word our high school had been locked down—no one was allowed to enter or leave. No additional information was available except that the school was locked down. After about two hours, the lock was lifted.

Almost immediately one of Clay's girl friends appeared at my door. Clay had brought a couple of guns and ammunition with him in his backpack when he went to school that morning. Thankfully, like most teenagers, he couldn't keep his deed secret, and he told this girl. She told a teacher. The teacher notified the administration.

During first period, Clay was called to the office. He was asked about the guns, and he admitted to having them. The school officer and principal escorted him to his locker, which he was ordered to open and step back from. The officer retrieved his backpack and found the guns and ammunition. Clay was arrested, and the school was locked down until they could be sure Clay had no accomplices and that there was no other danger.

MY RESPONSE

Clay was taken, I learned, to an adolescent psychiatric facility in the next town. Once his parents put me on the "approved visitor" list, I spent every Wednesday afternoon with Clay for the six weeks he was in the facility. Although I know he was receiving lots of group and individual counseling, he still seemed very willing to talk with me.

He had been taken off of all his medication and seemed to speak with a clarity I hadn't heard in years. He said he wasn't really sure why he brought the guns to school; he had not planned to hurt anyone there, but he had been considering killing himself later that day or perhaps the next. He showed the guns to the girl with the hope she would do exactly what she did. It was his last cry for help. His plan worked, and he began receiving the residential treatment he really needed.

We had some great talks over those weeks, and I assured him I would be at his hearing, which was quickly approaching. I thought I might be called as a character witness, but I was not. At the hearing, I witnessed one of the most difficult scenes I've ever endured in youth ministry.

Clay shuffled into the back of the courtroom, his feet shackled together. His hands were cuffed together in front of his body, held there by a chain around his waist. The room was crowded because several cases were to be heard that day. Clay walked by me, and I looked him in the eye, trying desperately to somehow assure him things would be okay. I was so shaken by seeing one of my youth in shackles I could hardly speak—though he was whisked by me so quickly, we had no time for words.

> Clay shuffled into the back of the courtroom, his feet shackled together. His hands were cuffed together in front of his body, held there by a chain around his waist. I was so shaken by seeing one of my youth in shackles I could hardly speak.

His case came up first, and the judge ordered the courtroom cleared. Because I had no official reason to be there, I had to leave, too. I never heard a word of his hearing, but it seemed to be fair. He was sentenced to finish high school in a secured facility in another state and then remain in custody until his 21st birthday. I didn't see him again until his release.

Clay returned to our city when his sentence was complete. He came by my office many times, and we talked for hours. He told of his years in state facilities; and, although one might think he would be bitter, he spoke very positively of the experience. He knew he needed help, and he really felt he got it. He loved most of his counselors, many of whom had been treated at similar facilities during their teenage years. He wanted to start attending the church and even asked if he could help with the youth group.

As much as I loved Clay, I must admit I wondered if he was really well or if he had simply timed out of the system. Could he be trusted alone with people? Was he safe? I knew he couldn't pass a background check and therefore wouldn't meet our Safe Sanctuary requirements. Still, I knew his past; he wasn't trying to hide it. I struggled between the grace and trust Jesus taught me to give and the fear and distrust the world had taught me. Which of these did I owe Clay?

I was planning to do a program with my group on cutting and self-mutilation, which I mentioned to Clay in one of our conversations. He admitted he had cut himself many times and then proceeded to roll up his sleeve to reveal scars on his arms. Suddenly, I knew how Clay could help with our youth group. I asked him if he would be willing to talk about his struggles and experience with cutting. He was glad to do so. For most of my youth, the topic of cutting seemed foreign. Had I presented the program alone that night, it would have remained foreign to them. Having Clay convey his story spoke volumes to our youth. Here was a real person from their high school who had struggled with this. The kids asked lots of questions, and Clay gave real and honest answers. It was a great evening.

A week or so later, Clay informed me he had a job offer in another town and would be moving there. He still struggles with a lot of things, but he now has the tools and knowledge to deal with them. He has a fairly strong relationship with Christ and usually leans on that knowledge. Still, from time to time, he stumbles a bit. All in all, though, I think Clay is going to turn out just fine.

IN RETROSPECT

If this situation reoccurred today, I would visit Clay just like I did before. Although there are certain restrictions, everyone in custody has a right to have visitors. Once his parents put me on the list, I could visit as often as I wanted. They would even bring Clay out of a group therapy session to visit with me.

I should have contacted the juvenile court to learn what the procedures of his hearing were going to be. I later learned the courtroom was only cleared so some confidential information could be presented. After about 45 minutes, everyone was allowed back in. Had I known the procedure, I could have stayed for the hearing.

Once he was incarcerated in another state, I felt I shouldn't write to him because I didn't think he could write back. (He was not allowed to have a pencil or other sharp object in his initial treatment). I assumed my writing to him might frustrate him since he could not write back. I learned that was not the case; he would have welcomed letters from home, and he could have written back.

Also, being "just a youth director," I felt somewhat inadequate to help Clay. I know now, he didn't need my professional help (he was getting that elsewhere). He needed my friendship. I didn't need to have the right words to say; I just needed to be there for him. Yes, I was there for him to a certain extent, but I could have been more available during some of the most difficult times.

QUESTIONS TO CONSIDER

In what ways can we create environments where troubled young people can grow in relationships that may help them later on during crises points in their lives?

How do we balance the needs of the 99 sheep in the fold with the one outlier who could consume much more time and attention?

What are the rules in my city, county, and state regarding contact with kids in the system? In what ways can relationships with officials in those areas be strengthened for such a time as this?

GOSSIP TRAIN
THE KID WHO FEEDS ON TALKING ABOUT OTHERS

Syler Thomas is a native Texan who has been the High School Pastor at Christ Church Lake Forest in Illinois since 1998. He writes a column for *Youthworker Journal*, has had articles published in *Leadership Journal* and the *Chicago Tribune*, and is the co-author of two books. He and his wife, Heidi, have four kids.

Teenagers love to gossip. So do pre-teens. And post-teens. Which would include adults…you and me. It's just that adults get a little more clever about it the older we get.

Sometimes it can come in the form of a "news update": "Have you heard the latest about Tammy? Well…"

Then there's the really spiritual way to do it, known as the "prayer concern": "We really need to be in prayer about the Thompsons. I heard…"

And don't forget the conversational loophole that allows you to say anything you wish about a person while avoiding the charge of gossip. It involves simply assuring your listeners how much you love the person in question. Then you can rip him to pieces: "Now don't get me wrong, I *love* Connor, I think he's a fantastic person. It's just that I can't *stand* it when…"

Along the same lines, if you're in the South, don't underestimate the power of the very effective "bless his heart": "That Jared, bless his heart, he is the dumbest fool on the planet."

You can put lipstick on a pig, but I'm not really sure why you'd want to do that. It's a waste of lipstick, and there's no use upsetting a perfectly good pig. The point is: gossip is gossip is gossip.

> You can put lipstick on a pig, but I'm not really sure why you'd want to do that. It's a waste of lipstick, and there's no use upsetting a perfectly good pig. The point is: gossip is gossip is gossip.

DILEMMAS

High schools are particularly fertile breeding grounds for gossip—veritable Petri dishes for this particularly destructive behavior. And for many students, pointing out gossip is kind of like trying to talk to a fish about water. It's constantly around them, so they don't really notice it. If you offered 100 students a thousand dollars each to go a week without gossiping, I think 95 wouldn't be able to do it—and the other five would probably have to stop speaking completely for the entire week in order to pull it off.

As leaders, however, sometimes it's our job to sit around and talk about students behind their backs. Parents come to us with concerns about their students. We go to our volunteer leaders to share information so that they can adequately

39

be brought up to speed on a student's situation. Most of the time, we are *just* on the "appropriate" side of "not gossip"—but walking that line can be very tricky.

The situation where I've seen this come into play the most involves students who talk to me about what they see their friends doing outside of youth group settings.

In my first year of ministry, a well-meaning student approached me with some information about another student. "Syler, I feel like I need to tell you something about Jenny that I think you should know." I felt that twinge of hesitation, wondering whether this was a good idea or not.

MY RESPONSE

I decided to let him tell me. He proceeded to talk about a party that he attended where he had seen Jenny openly and unashamedly consuming alcohol. I'm not sure what he thought I would do with that information. Jenny did not come from a churched home, and it actually didn't surprise me that she was drinking. I wasn't even sure whether she was a Christian or not.

That incident forced me to consider further how I would respond to that kind of information in the future. I vowed that from that point on, I would choose to avoid listening to that kind of gossip, even when it was couched from a standpoint of concern for the person's wellbeing. After all, what was I supposed to do with that information? Approach the student and tell her that I heard she was drinking? I didn't—and I still don't—want to create a culture of tattling, where students either feel like they're constantly being watched and reported or are expected to watch and report.

> I don't want to create a culture of tattling, where students either feel like they're constantly being watched and reported or are expected to watch and report.

IN RETROSPECT

In this situation, the student in question (Jenny) was a brand new believer, or perhaps not even a believer—so she was acting consistently with her beliefs. I am a firm believer that it's ineffective to try to address behavior modification without going after the heart first. Because this student was not a committed believer and hadn't asked to be held accountable for her actions, I ended up ignoring the information I had been given and trusted in the work of the Holy Spirit to bring about repentance in due time.

I do believe standards are different for committed students who ask to be held accountable, and I am willing to act in that role to some degree. I still don't listen to gossip about them, though. Each August on my student ministry team retreat, I talk about the expectations I have for each of them, including abstaining from drugs and alcohol, and to be above reproach in regard to sexual activity. I then tell them that I am not able to be their babysitter, nor do I want to be. And I don't want students to come to me to report on a violator.

I read Galatians 6:1 to them: "If someone is caught in a sin, you who live by the Spirit should restore that person gently" (NIV), and explain that it's actually *their* job to confront the sin. We talk about what it means to confront and rebuke, and about how to receive that in love. I then tell them that if they are unwilling to confront some sin in a brother or sister's life, that's okay; but the alternative should not be to gossip about it.

PUTTING THE SCRIPTURES INTO PRACTICE

This is a very simple application of what Jesus talks about in Matthew 18:15-17. By definition, gossip ignores the concept that Jesus lays out, which is: If you have a problem with someone, go to that person directly and work it out. Sharing this passage—or Proverbs 16:28: "a gossip separates close friends"— can help young people realize that when they gossip, they aren't just engaging in harmless chitchat; they are disobeying Scripture.

So how do we help students put a stop to gossip as it's happening? I'll never forget the time I saw this modeled perfectly. I was in a small group of six people, and one person began sharing a bit too much about a mutual friend. If no one had said anything to stop it, a gossip session would have ensued. My friend Brian calmly, but firmly, said, "I don't really want to talk about that." It was awkward for a couple of seconds, and then someone brought up another subject.

I tell that story to students all the time. If you have a say in the matter, you don't need to cause a scene, call someone out, or make anyone feel uncomfortable. Just say, "I don't really want to talk about that." Then trust that the conversation will move in a different direction.

EXCEPTIONS

Situations arise when your desire to avoid gossip is superseded by other factors, especially when they involve the wellbeing of a student. Many years back, a student made on offhand comment to me about how he had seen another student (whose parents attend our church) with a large amount of marijuana in his room and suspected he was dealing. I hated that he had told me, but I knew that I couldn't sit on this information. I made a quick phone call to the parent of the student in question, saying that I couldn't prove that the information was true, that students sometimes exaggerate or are misinformed, but I thought they should know.

She called me later to tell me how grateful she was that I had contacted her, and that because of my tip, she was able to put a stop to the situation. Why was this an exception? Because the situation seemed extreme enough (this wasn't one-time or "experimental" drug use) that to do nothing seemed negligent.

POSITIVE GOSSIP?

We should keep the positive stuff quiet, too. Even when we are reporting on *good* things in a student's life, we have to be careful that we don't over share. What may be no big deal to us may be an incredibly big deal to a young person; and because kids trust us with so much of their lives, we have no right to decide what we should share about them to others.

For instance, if a student privately professes to me that he has put his faith in Jesus for the first time, I shouldn't share that information with other students. Word can quickly spread about that kind of thing, and the student could feel like a confidence has been broken if he hears students talking about what was supposed to be a private matter. Encourage the student himself to share that information, and if you feel compelled to share the story with your staff, don't share the student's name.

> Leaders have to model that we don't want to be a part of gossip.

The bottom line is that we as leaders have to model that we don't want to be a part of gossip, and then we have to follow through on it, even though our curiosity may prompt us otherwise—bless their hearts or not.

QUESTIONS TO CONSIDER

In what ways do I gossip about others? What is my motive? How can I break that habit?

In what ways do I allow others' gossip to flourish around me? How can I nicely, but firmly, begin changing the dynamics in those relationships so I don't feed the gossip beast?

How can I actively begin changing the DNA of the entire ministry so that gossip is not the norm?

THE CRIMINAL
THE KID FACING CHARGES

Susan Groce worked with the youth at her home church for ten years before accepting a call in 2008 to serve the Cumberland Presbyterian Denomination as the Coordinator of Ministries with Youth and Young Adults. She lives in Collierville, Tennessee, with her husband, Jaime, and two boys, Braxton and Thatcher.

I was serving at church camp when I received the call from home. Ryan and Kasey, two youth in my church, had been involved in a car accident. Ryan had been drinking. Kasey had not. Ryan was in the hospital. Kasey had been killed.

My heart sank. I had just spent a weekend with them at a retreat where Kasey and I had engaged in a meaningful conversation about faith, and I was thankful for the time we had together. I quickly got to the hospital where Ryan had recently been moved to a private room. Ryan was in no condition to talk, but his family indicated that charges against him were possible.

> Ryan had been drinking. Kasey had not. Ryan was in the hospital. Kasey had been killed.

As I left the hospital, I received a call from Kasey's mother. She asked if I would perform the funeral service. I accepted and spent the next three days working with and ministering to Kasey's family in preparation for her service and burial.

The funeral was held on a Friday morning. Ryan, having been released from the hospital, was present. But his presence was not without anxiety from Kasey's friends and family. They held Ryan 100% responsible for Kasey's death, and after the funeral they sought legal counsel to pursue criminal and civil action against him and his family.

One month later, Ryan was arrested and formally charged with involuntary manslaughter. I was asked by his counsel to testify on Ryan's behalf.

Kasey's family made it known, through mutual friends, that they were unhappy about my decision; though no communication was directly with me.

DILEMMAS

Certainly, Ryan's choice to drink and then to drive was a poor one. He abused the trust given to him by his parents, Kasey's parents, and his friends.

Though these families were on opposing sides, I wanted to minister to both. Both Ryan and Kasey were active in the youth group.

Though this chain of events dramatically impacted the rest of the youth group, some of Ryan's friends continued illegal and self-destructive behavior in the time surrounding and immediately following this incident. I needed to make sure that my testimony could not translate into approval of what Ryan had done and the activities that led to the incident. On the other hand, I wanted to follow Jesus' example in extending grace and love to Ryan and his family.

MY RESPONSE

I agreed to testify on Ryan's behalf. When questioned, I provided information on Ryan's character. I truly thought he was remorseful for what he had done, and believed him when he said that part of his life was behind him. As I was on the stand, I looked into the faces of Kasey's parents. The pain they felt from losing their only daughter permeated the courtroom.

Ryan's trial lasted two days with verdict and sentencing two weeks later. At the verdict, it was discovered that Ryan had failed the drug test given to him during the trial. What would have been a verdict of probation with community service became a two-year sentence in Juvenile Jail.

> I had testified on his behalf, and he had betrayed me just like he had betrayed everyone else. I tried to minister to both families, and the whole thing had blown up in my face. I felt like a failure.

I was upset when we left the courtroom. I was angry with Ryan for drinking. I was angry with him for using drugs. But most of all, I was angry with him for putting me in a situation where I looked like a liar. I had testified on his behalf, and he had betrayed me just like he had betrayed everyone else. I tried to minister to both families, and the whole thing had blown up in my face. I felt like a failure.

Ryan was transported to jail. There was a brief waiting period with background and reference checks and court approval before I could visit him. That gave me time to "cool off" from my anger and disappointment in the outcome of his trial. When I saw him for the first time since the courtroom, he was nervous. I said, "Ryan, I'm not mad at you. At least, not anymore."

"I was worried you would be," he replied.

"Ryan, what happened?"

"Ms. Susan, I made some terrible choices. I am responsible for what I did. Now, I have to pay the price."

"You know that we still love you, and most of all that God will always love you."

We went on to talk about his plans for his time in prison and what his goals were when he got out; but most of our time was spent in prayer. I visited Ryan once a month, most often with others in his family or approved visitors from the church.

In the end, Ryan served 18 months for his crime. He graduated from high school in prison. After he completed his sentence, he enrolled in college, got married, had a child, and recently divorced. Ryan and his family left the church. They couldn't bear the knowledge of the past that remained in the congregation.

I tried contacting Kasey's family after the trial, but my efforts were not returned. Almost one year after her death, I received a letter from Kasey's mother. She was hurt. She was hurt that I had testified on Ryan's behalf. She felt I had betrayed her and Kasey.

The civil case Kasey's family filed was later dropped.

Kasey's family moved, and I heard they've become involved in a local congregation and continue to take life one day at a time.

IN RETROSPECT

I would have stayed in closer contact with Kasey's family during the trial. Even though they knew I was going to testify, I should have told them myself and discussed my reasons for testifying on Ryan's behalf. I allowed their anger towards Ryan, his family, and me to talk myself into giving them time and space. That time drove a wedge between the church and Kasey's family that integrated feelings of betrayal. I never responded to her letter. I felt justified because the letter was accusatory and didn't ask for a response. I wish I had responded.

The congregation showed love and grace to both families and still does. Though both families chose to leave, I see the congregation could have done no better during the entire situation.

Charges brought against any young person, for any reason, are tough. They disappoint and cause loss of trust, but ultimately they can be the rock bottom needed to turn a life around.

QUESTIONS TO CONSIDER

In what ways does our worldly desire for justice sometimes cloud our ability to be Christ-like to those who make bad decisions?

50 IT HAPPENS

What biblical, theological, and moral issues are at stake when we try to minister to warring factions within our congregations? How can we minimize some of the conflict? And what do we do if one side or the other will not relent?

When we attempt to balance justice, mercy, grace, and truth, do we have tendencies to lean toward one at the expense of another? How can we help ensure we are serving as God's hands and feet rather than expressions of our own natural proclivities?

ASSERTIVE
YET INVITING
DISCIPLINE AT CHURCH

Jack Radcliffe has served young people and their families for more than 20 years in churches in Ohio, Michigan, Massachusetts, and Tennessee. Jack currently serves as adjunct professor of Educational Ministry at Martin Methodist College and is the Dean of The Youth Ministry Institute of the Tennessee Conference of the United Methodist Church. In addition, he is a ministry trainer, speaker, and president of Redwood Coaching, redwoodcoach.com.

At the beginning of my 17th year in youth ministry, I embarked on a new journey with a new church. The youth ministry had a history of having to deal with difficult situations created by students and leaders on trips. My first order of business at the new church was to address an incident that took place a couple of months before I arrived. At the fall retreat, a group of high school boys took part in what had become a retreat ritual: hanging out in their cabin naked. Apparently, this ritual (called "Naked Time") had been passed on over time, completely unknown to the staff and leaders.

On this particular weekend, the ritual took place as usual. An attempt to initiate a freshman, however, didn't go so well. He was reluctant to participate. A young, well-meaning leader who walked into the situation tried to alleviate the young boy's embarrassment. His effort failed miserably and led to the church being alerted by unhappy parents. Temporary action was taken, but it was decided to let the new youth pastor decide what to do. Parents and church leaders both expected assurance that "Naked Time" wouldn't happen again.

My hopes of reversing the tide of having to deal with "trip issues" were dashed several months later. Over the course of the two-week domestic mission trip, we sent three students home because of suicidal threats and other emotional issues.

> Establishing boundaries involves a delicate dance between ensuring relational and physical safety, not making involvement in the youth group suffocating to students, and not making it hard for leaders to enforce the boundaries.

The next summer I learned after returning home from a mission trip to Central America that several leaders purchased beer and drank it on the roof of our hotel during the end of the trip R&R.

DILEMMAS

One of the first things a youth pastor learns how to do is establish boundaries for the youth ministry. Establishing boundaries involves a delicate dance

53

between ensuring relational and physical safety, not making involvement in the youth group suffocating to students, and not making it hard for leaders to enforce the boundaries. My own dance resulted in the crafting of three simple rules:

1. Respect one another.
2. Respect the property we are using.
3. Respect the people with whom we come into contact.

After unpacking and reinforcing the rules by teaching their biblical foundations and the consequences for violating them, we enjoyed a culture of personal responsibility and mutual regard. Issues were few, but when they occurred, each was handled individually. This approach served me well for 16 years in several churches. However, the world was changing rapidly, and new approaches to keeping youth safe were required.

Prior to my first day in the office at First Church, I received a multi-page document of youth ministry guidelines. Discussions about the policies with volunteers and staff revealed how this church chose to respond. Many of the youth ministry policies were developed in response to incidents that occurred on youth ministry trips.

Clearly, parents and church leaders wanted assurance that we would do all we could to prevent our young people from making choices that resulted in behavior that was dangerous to themselves and the group. Equally clearly, I had gone about accomplishing this over the past 17 years in a far different manner than the new church I was serving.

We agreed that youth ministry staff and leaders were responsible to God along with family and the church to feed and protect our young people. I felt that we were also responsible to honor the developmental needs of young people: specifically, that we help them grow from being externally motivated and controlled to being internally driven. But this journey of gradually loosening the boundaries promises mistakes and failure along the way, and I was more okay with that than the church was.

I had to decide how to balance all of these responsibilities, honor the adolescent journey, *and* deal with the gap between how I handled the setting and violation of boundaries, and the way the church had become accustomed. The pressure to ensure expected student behavior would be a tall order.

HOW I RESPONDED

Feeling the need to assimilate into the new culture (and keep my job), I set aside my preferences and crafted policies addressing each of the situations we encountered. Students were to wear clothing at all times in public dorm and cabin areas, and leaders were not to shower or change at the same time as students. Leaders were also not permitted to sleep in the same room as students. An extensive mission trip application and interview process was developed and implemented to sniff out emotional issues students may have. We reserved the right to refuse someone participation based on our findings. It also had to be spelled out in our policies that leaders could not drink on trips.

All the while I worked on trying to change the culture of policymaking to the development of personal responsibility and mutual regard. Efforts to put practices in place to help students develop an internal center of control were often met with skepticism. The good news is that my last trip three years after my first with this church proceeded without incident. The bad news is, students overall didn't seem to be any better at making wise choices on their own than the day I arrived.

> All the while I worked on trying to change the culture of policymaking to the development of personal responsibility and mutual regard.

IN RETROSPECT

Looking back, I realize that in my attempt to use the external control policy-making approach of the church *and* my preference of helping students become internally controlled, I did not set us up for success. These two obviously opposite approaches to handling the issue could not work together at the same time. If I could do it over again, I would take the risk of implementing my approach. Accompanied by a lot of communication with parents and church leaders and training of leaders, I believe this would be a win.

QUESTIONS TO CONSIDER

When complicated issues arise, is my first tendency to deal with that issue specifically, or is it to craft a new policy? Why do I have that tendency? In what ways is it helpful? In what ways is it frustrating?

Do my boss and other ministry leadership respond the same way that I do, or does that become an additional source of conflict? If unlike responses, how can I help minimize the conflict?

How well am I balancing the "delicate dance" of boundaries and hospitality? How can I get better?

ALCOHOL
WHEN PARENTS ENCOURAGE UNDERAGE CONSUMPTION

Hank Hilliard is a 17-year youth ministry veteran. Hank serves as the Director of Youth Ministries for Franklin First UMC. He spent four years as the Director of Young People's Ministries for the General Board of Discipleship. He is the author of *The Leadership Lab*, a DVD-based resource for high school youth and *Re-Entry*, a resource for debriefing and applying your short-term mission trip to everyday life.

It was a fragile situation that was teetering on the verge of chaos. More than 100 young people had descended upon the church gymnasium preparing to depart on our annual youth retreat to Florida. In tow were another 200 or so parents and siblings.

Families were paying last minute balances, stacking up their bags, and filling out forms that were supposed to have been turned in weeks before. Parents were busy offering the adult volunteers and me words of encouragement, giving their kids last minute instructions, and discussing plans with one another about how they would spend the five days with their kids out of the house.

Older youth were attacking me with questions about which bus they were on and whom they would be rooming with while the younger youth were so consumed with excitement and anticipation that they were just running around the gym. Many preparations still lay ahead, and we only had about 45 minutes until we were scheduled to board the buses.

I felt a tap on my shoulder. I turned to see my associate, Steve, looking very anxious. He said in a very serious tone, "I need to talk to you." I knew it was important because at our adult meeting only an hour before we had agreed that we would not pull one another from our assigned tasks unless something important came up that we could not handle on our own.

We walked into the hallway and around a corner to escape the noise and have some semblance of privacy. Steve leaned in and said in a very serious tone, "Austin is drunk."

Austin was a rising senior who had been an active member of our youth ministry since eighth grade. He was a good kid, but he made an abundance of bad decisions. Austin worked hard to be tough and cared a little too much about being cool. He was one of those teenagers who drive youth pastors crazy: a young man with unmatched potential; a natural leader, but either did not recognize this gift or just did not care to use this gift to be a positive influence on others. To make things more difficult, Austin's parents were on the verge of divorce.

DILEMMA

My immediate reaction was anger. I thought, *How could he do this to me? Surely he knows this is putting me in a terrible position.* I wanted to send him home. Actually, I was so mad I didn't even want to look at him or talk to him. I wanted Steve to send him home.

My face was flushed, and my mind was racing trying to process this information and figure out some way to even begin to make a decision. Steve was not only my associate but also a long-time friend. As if reading my mind he continued, "I know you want to send him home, but I think we should talk about this before you make a decision."

My mind screamed, *Discuss this? Discuss what? He is drunk. Get that disrespectful, self-centered kid out of here.* Fortunately I had yet to open my mouth. Finally, I asked Steve to tell me what happened and how he found out Austin was drunk.

Steve explained that he greeted Austin in the parking lot. Austin gave him a head nod and stumbled past him into the hallway outside the gymnasium. He saw Austin stumble over to some friends, put his arms around them, and begin laughing and joking. Steve was suspicious and approached Austin. He got close enough to realize that Austin smelled of alcohol, so he pulled Austin aside privately and confronted him. Austin confessed that he had been drinking, at which point Steve sent Austin into my office with two other adult volunteers waiting for me to arrive to talk with him.

MY RESPONSE

Steve and I walked down the hall towards the office. My mind was in overdrive, and my heart pounded with anxiousness and anger. Susan, a volunteer who was sitting with Austin, saw us approaching and came into the hall just outside the door. Susan was a veteran volunteer with one son in the youth ministry and another who had graduated the youth ministry and was now a volunteer himself. She was also a close friend of Austin's mom. Before I could even say a word Susan said, "I think you should let him go on the trip."

I shook my head. "How can I let a drunk kid go on a retreat?" I thought about the consequences: the loss of authority and respect, complaints from second-guessing parents, an early morning appointment with my senior pastor.

I asked Steve what he thought. Steve said, "I think we should let him go, too."

ALCOHOL **61**

Now I felt ganged up on. *Easy for you to say*, I thought, *I am the one in charge, and I'll be the one to catch the blame if something goes wrong.* But all I could say was, "Okay." Then I told them I needed to talk to Austin alone.

I entered the office and sat to talk with Austin, while Steve and Susan took over my duties of greeting people and organizing the check-in process. I was angry, and I let Austin know it. I don't really remember what I said, but I am sure if I wrote it down that it would not read like a Hallmark greeting card. When I was done with my rant, I asked him for an explanation.

Austin said his dad had brought home some new brand of beer he was excited about and he wanted Austin to drink it with him.

My anger towards Austin lifted a bit as it shifted full-force towards his father. I told Austin to stay put. I walked to an empty part of the parking lot and called his dad. I reported the situation and told him of Austin's claim that he was the one responsible for giving him the beer. The father confirmed that it was true. No remorse. Clueless to how wrong this was on so many levels.

Austin's mom was serving as a cook on the retreat. She was already at the beach with the other cooks preparing for us to arrive in a few hours. I called her. She had not heard any of this yet, so I filled her in. I informed her I was trying to decide what to do with Austin and had about ten minutes before I had to go inside and give my send-off speech to the parents and get everyone loaded on the buses. She began crying and pled with me, "Please, let him come on the trip. Please do not make him go home to his father. Austin needs this trip. Austin needs you and the youth group. I will do anything."

After I got off the phone with Austin's mom, I pulled together Steve and Susan. Since they were both so involved, I felt I needed to consult with them before I decided. Not surprisingly they both still felt he should be allowed to go on the trip. Grudgingly, I consented.

I returned to the office to find Austin where I had left him. I told him that I wanted to send him home but that I was not going to because Steve and Susan had fought for him and won me over. I told him that he could get on the bus if he agreed to the following conditions. He would be sent home immediately if I heard him or any of his buddies joking about this or if any middle school kids began talking about how cool he was. (That last part doesn't really make sense to me now, but I did say it.) I added that in addition to following all the usual trip rules that he would be required to be five minutes early to every meal, program, and activity and that he better be in his bed at lights-out. I closed by saying, "It's your decision. Agree to those conditions, and you can get on the bus. If you don't think you can do that, stay here." I got up and walked inside to make my send-off speech.

After my speech, some final announcements, and a send off prayer, we all climbed aboard the buses. Austin quietly and inconspicuously picked up his bag and boarded the bus. As the buses pulled out of the parking lot, I called Austin's mom to let her know her son was coming with us.

> A serious decision, a short window of time, and a gym full of more than 100 youth and adult leaders and their families feverishly preparing to depart for a five-day trip to the beach. It was a perfect storm.

This was one of the toughest situations I have dealt with in ministry. A serious decision, a short window of time, and a gym full of more than 100 youth and adult leaders and their families feverishly preparing to depart for a five-day trip to the beach. It was a perfect storm.

IN RETROSPECT

In looking back at this situation more than five years later I have learned a few things. Some of the things I did were positive:

1. I did not act until I had all the vital information. My first reaction was to blow up at Austin and tell him to never come back. All I knew was that he was drunk and I felt hurt and angry. If I had done this, I would have pushed Austin away and probably hurt his mother and Steve and Susan who were all stakeholders in what happened to Austin and deserved to have some say in the outcome. Speaking with Austin and both of his parents first was a huge help in making a well-informed decision.

2. I sought the opinions of others. Although the ultimate decision rested on my shoulders, I brought others in to help make the decision. In this case, I actually went along with Steve and Susan even though I disagreed with it. I realize now that the reason I wanted to send Austin home had very little to do with Austin and much more to do with myself. I thought allowing him to go would undermine my authority and make me vulnerable to attack.

3. I trusted my other leaders. Susan and Steve were both very steadfast in their belief that Austin should go on the trip. I listened to their reasons with an open mind.

I did not handle this situation perfectly, though. If I could go back in time, I would do some things differently:

1. I would involve the senior pastor. My pastor had empowered me to make many decisions, and I feel confident this was a situation when he would let me make the call and support my decision. However, pastors do not like surprises. I am sure that rumors circulated around the church while we were gone, and one phone call could have set off a chain of events that could have blown up in my face. Fortunately, my pastor was on vacation at the time, and no one called him. When we got back from the trip, I sent him an email letting him know what happened and that everything turned out okay. I never heard anything from him or anyone else in the church about it. Miraculously it all passed calmly and quietly, but that easily could have not been the case.

2. I would have kept my emotions in check when first talking with Austin. I tore into him pretty good, and I could have really damaged my relationship with him. Once again, fortunately Austin either had a thick enough skin or a big enough heart to not check out of our relationship.

THE REST OF THE STORY

Like a good family comedy, everything worked out fine. We had an amazing retreat, and Austin lived up to our agreement. Austin's mother was relieved to have her son with her. Years later, Austin called me from college. I had sent him a birthday card, and he called to thank me. During that call, he said something that I will never forget. He said, "Hank, you were the only adult in my life who didn't want something from me. You just wanted to be my friend." I realized then that many adults had probably given up on Austin. If I had sent him home that night he probably would have felt like I, and the other leaders at the church had, too.

Austin graduated from college with honors and is now serving his country in the Marine Corps. Although his parents did finally divorce, Austin remains close to both of them, especially his mother. Every now and then, I get a Facebook message from Austin just checking in to see how I am doing, and I remember why God dragged me into this crazy calling of youth ministry.

QUESTIONS TO CONSIDER

Am I "slow to anger," or do I have a tendency to fly off the handle? In what ways can I avoid making rash decisions, even when the decision-making window is very short?

In order to be more likely to make wise choices, who are in my "multitude of counselors" with whom to discuss difficult decisions?

Who are all of the key leaders in my church who need to be notified in case of difficult decisions (immediate supervisor, senior pastor, lay leader, personnel, committee chair, etc.), and what are the media through which—and the processes by which—those people should be informed when making decisions on the run?

What responsibilities do I have in a situation like this beyond just whether or not the kid goes on the trip? What needs to happen between the church leadership and grossly inappropriate parental decisions, like Dad's promotion of underage drinking?

BEYOND THONGS AND MIDRIFFS
DRESS CODE FOR THE 21ST CENTURY

Dixon Kinser is a husband, father, speaker, author, musician, amateur filmmaker and Episcopal priest. He works in youth and young adult ministry, rides his bike when he can and takes movies and TV way too seriously. Dixon is the author of *Exploring Blue Like Jazz* with Donald Miller and lives with his family in Nashville, Tennessee.

During a mission trip one summer, our group's flight schedule required us to stay overnight at a hotel. This particular hotel had a pool, and although we did not swim often as a youth group, I thought some pool time would be a great opportunity to unwind after a week of service work. My policy for events like this has always been for girls to avoid wearing two-piece swimsuits and boys to avoid wearing Speedos. These standards are communicated up front and were certainly included in this trip's materials.

Imagine my surprise, then, when Kathy, one of our senior girls, walked onto the pool deck wearing not just a two-piece, but a string bikini. As she strode confidently over to join our group in the water, the guys watched her walk in what seemed like slow motion—though the cheesy background music, back lighting, and wind to blow her hair were missing, the scene was still right out of a teen movie. Meanwhile, I was fighting a mix of incredulity, shock, and offense as my feelings of "How dare she?" gave way to, "How do I handle this?"

As casually as I could, I swam over to her and quietly asked if she had seen the dress code restrictions on the packing list. She responded firmly and bluntly,

"Yeah, I saw it, but I think it's crap and not fair! Two-piece swimsuits are in fashion right now, and that's all I have to wear. So, why can't I wear one? If the reason I can't wear a two-piece is because the guys can't control themselves, then that's their problem and not mine. Why is their self-control my responsibility?"

> If the reason I can't wear a two-piece is because the guys can't control themselves, then that's their problem and not mine.

"Ummm..." I said, stammering to craft a defense. Not noticing, she continued over me,

"Speedos are not in fashion for guys, so your dress code doesn't require any sacrifice for them at all, while for me it does. It's a double standard! Why

68 IT HAPPENS

do women always have to change to deal with male weaknesses? When is some of this their responsibility?"

Taking all this in, I didn't know what to do next. This was not because I believed Kathy was right to wear her two-piece in defiance of my dress code (she wasn't). But there was more to her critique of my policy than just someone who wanted to look sexy. Kathy had rightly identified some of the very real misogynist undertones that lurk around modesty conversations in our culture. She had also appropriately (albeit accidentally) challenged me to address these matters; not in the language of rules, but in the Christian vernacular of relationship. So what should I do next? The answer can be found, oddly enough, in an ancient conversation about meat.

DILEMMAS

In 1 Corinthians 8-10, Paul addresses a pressing theological question this young church asks him: Can they eat meat that has been sacrificed to idols or not? While this may sound like a simple question, it isn't. Wrapped within the "idol meat" question are many of the larger problems the Corinthian church was struggling with, and Paul takes the opportunity to tackle both.

The Corinthian church was made up of a broad spectrum of classes and races. They struggled to not bring their culture's class divisions into the common life of the church, but the idol meat issue was one of the areas in which they were failing. Eating meat in the ancient world was not something that happened very often unless one was rich. Part of living and working in the upper tiers of Corinthian society meant attending civic functions where meat (that had been sacrificed in worship to one of the many gods in Corinth) was served for dinner. The wait staff for such a dinner would be made up of servants from the lower rungs of the class ladder, which made it entirely likely that two members of the Corinthian church would be at the same dinner with one eating and the other serving.

But imagine that one of the servants at the dinner were a new convert to Jesus Christ, and imagine (as was often the case) that he struggled to give up his old ways of worshipping idols. What would he think when he saw another, more mature, member of his church eating meat that had been devoted to one such idol? He might be confused into thinking that said leader was worshiping that idol. Consequently, he might be tempted to take up old idolatrous patterns because one of his church leaders appeared to be doing the same.

BEYOND THONGS AND MIDRIFFS   **69**

Some felt as if that was simply the servant's problem. After all, are not the wise church leaders free to eat idol meat because of their freedom in Christ? They seemed to think so, and they wanted Paul to affirm their convictions—and he does…sort of.

Paul first acknowledges that false gods are not real; therefore, food sacrificed to them cannot defile a person (1 Cor 8:4-6, 8). In theory, then, one is free to eat meat sacrificed to these gods because of Jesus and his lordship over all false rulers. However, Paul continues to explain that if a person's exercise of "freedom" causes someone else to struggle, that person should stop:

> But take care that this liberty of yours does not somehow become a stumbling block to the weak. For if others see you, who possess knowledge, eating in the temple of an idol, might they not, since their conscience is weak, be encouraged to the point of eating food sacrificed to idols? So by your knowledge those weak believers for whom Christ died are destroyed. But when you thus sin against members of your family, and wound their conscience when it is weak, you sin against Christ. Therefore, if food is a cause of their falling, I will never eat meat, so that I may not cause one of them to fall.
>
> —1 Corinthians 8:9-13

True freedom, Paul contends, comes from laying down one's rights for the sake of someone else rather than being permitted to do whatever one desires. This is the true practice and pattern of love exemplified by Jesus himself. After all, Paul seems to say in verse 13, "Jesus died for you, and you won't change your diet?! Please!"

"Jesus died for you, and you won't change your diet?! Please!"

Even though the idol meat issue could have been answered simply, Paul recognizes the larger issue underneath the Corinthians' question and takes the opportunity to remind this church who they are and whose they are. At stake was this community's ability (or inability) to demonstrate in their relationships what God is like. As such, their practice of "freedom" did not embody Jesus' pattern of self-emptying love but instead the cultural practice of vanity. Christian freedom is not doing what we want; it is giving up our rights for someone else's benefit. That is how Jesus did it, and that is how we are called to live.

HOW I RESPONDED

1 Corinthians 8 (and the remainder of the argument in 9 and 10) is a great corollary for my dress code quandary. In the same way the idol meat situation was illustrative of more significant struggles in the Corinthian church, so too was Kathy's challenge to my dress code. Hers was not a simple question of what the rules said she could wear. It was instead a question about how to be our brother's and sister's keeper and live Jesus' command to love as He loved us. If I didn't address that, I would have missed both an opportunity and the point.

Ultimately, I upheld my policy regarding two-piece swimsuits. I admitted to Kathy that it was indeed because some of our guys will sexualize her if she wears a bikini. I also pointed out that the policy exists not because bikinis are inherently "against God" but because, like the "idol meat," they had the potential to damage the relationships of our group members. Because I was calling for this relational ethic, though, I also had to challenge our guys to abstain from the violent cultural forces that pornographize all women and groom us to do the same. I also challenged myself to consider if, as a pastor, avoiding poolside events for a time was a way to love both my girls and my boys until we'd had a chance to talk and pray through these dynamics.

I didn't say any of this until afterward, though. In the moment I was so taken aback I just said, "Well, I'll have to think about it and tell you later," which ended up being the best thing to do. Because Kathy's relationship to our community mattered as much as anyone else's, if I had made an example of her in that moment or just put my foot down it would have generated more heat than light. Some moments require a stubborn, principled stand; but most of the time, dress code is not one of them.

Fortunately, our community's conversation about dress codes has not stopped at swimsuits. When we noticed that church was the only place we were free from the ubiquity of advertisements, we took up the discipline of avoiding clothes with brand labels on them. When we do it we always note that wearing a corporate logo on a T-shirt is not intrinsically wrong—but for the health of our common life, we choose to lay down this right as an act of love. This is a small way we can take up our crosses and follow Jesus into the life of the new creation.

QUESTIONS TO CONSIDER

What are the hallmarks of your ministry's dress code, and why were those policies adopted? What do those policies say about your underlying philosophies of human behavior?

Which freedoms do you or your students intentionally choose to avoid in order to create a safer place for others who are new to faith? Which ones should you choose to avoid?

When confronted with inconsistencies or perceived unfairness in policies, how do you find the balance between firmly enforcing the boundaries and searching for the underlying issues?

THE BIG TRIP QUESTION
TO SEND HIM HOME
OR NOT TO SEND HIM HOME?

Karen Jones served as a youth minister for more than 15 years in Missouri and Texas. She has led conferences,; written youth ministry curriculum, numerous articles, and book chapters;, and engaged in research with adolescents and youth ministers throughout her professional career. She is Chair of the Department of Ministry and Missions at Huntington University in Indiana.

I was just completing my first year at the large, affluent, urban church. As is often the case when following a much-loved former youth minister, I had experienced some resistance in being accepted by the older youth during that time.

The group had a tradition of attending a summer camp with several other churches from the region, so we continued that practice the first summer I was there. It was an eye-opening experience for the adult volunteers who went along as chaperones for the first time, as they encountered other adults who were teaching things that contradicted the church's doctrine. I vividly remember coming across the father of one of our students one night, a deacon at our church, who was sitting alone on a bench in the middle of the college campus where we were staying. He was weeping openly as he lamented the fact that the church had been sending their youth there, year after year, without ever realizing how they were being indoctrinated.

We did not attend that camp the next year, much to the initial distress of those older youth. The fact that I was leading a break with tradition was an obstacle to overcome, so the pastor encouraged me to plan our own camp, one that would be so appealing to our students that they wouldn't mind missing the old experience. So that is exactly what we did.

Our camp was held in the Rocky Mountains, and it included rafting, a high ropes course, and rappelling, in addition to other recreational opportunities and an all-star team of speakers and worship leaders. I covered all the bases in terms of informational meetings, medical releases, and parental permissions.

There was some concern about the behavior of a few of the senior high males, who sometimes crossed the line with their partying and risk-taking. In fact, some of the adult volunteers wondered whether or not we should allow them to attend. I didn't want to exclude any students, however, on the basis of their past actions, and I thought their desire to attend the camp was a positive sign.

The camp would be a great opportunity to speak into their lives and perhaps help them rearrange their lives' directions and priorities. I did, however, make it clear to everyone that there would be a zero-tolerance policy in terms of drug use, including alcohol. The parents actually signed a form that listed the rules, agreeing to pay for an airline ticket if their child had to be sent home for violating the zero-tolerance policy.

DILEMMAS

The students were in awe of the location of the camp and responded positively to worship. The "partiers" were model campers, and it seemed that we were finally turning a corner in the ministry. Our first crisis was a broken arm. We soon discovered that this was a typical occurrence with this particular student, who apparently had brittle bones. (Who knew? Something to add to the medical information form next time.) His parents weren't overly concerned, and one trip to the hospital didn't dampen our spirits. He came back with a cast that made him a camp star. Unfortunately, that wasn't our only crisis.

The worship leader was rooming with some of our older male students: the partiers and risk-takers included. One morning, after the students were off to small groups, he approached me with a concern. He had noticed some odd behavior from three of the boys when he entered the room that morning; some of their comments and actions sent off alarms. When they left the room, he went to the trashcan and opened up the empty Mountain Dew bottles they had deposited. The strong smell of alcohol coming out of the bottles was the reason he had approached me. There was no mistaking it: the boys had obviously been drinking, and not just that morning. The bottles had been accumulating. My heart sank.

> There was no mistaking it: the boys had obviously been drinking, and not just that morning. The bottles had been accumulating.

MY RESPONSE

Accompanied by the worship leader, I confronted the three students with our discovery. They readily admitted that they had been drinking ever since they had arrived. Apparently, one of the boys had the ingenious idea of pouring Zima into the Mountain Dew bottles before they loaded the buses for the trip, and the other two boys went along with the plan. They knew they had broken the rules, but didn't appear remorseful for what they had done, just that they had been discovered. They also knew that the rules said they would be sent home, but I don't think they expected it. We talked with them at length and prayed with them, then asked each of them to call their parents. I rounded up the volunteers and let them know what had been happening, and I consulted with the pastor via telephone.

While the rules had been clearly established, I never expected that I would actually have to fly anyone home—and I'll admit, I resented being put into the situation. As if the dilemma could be any worse, one of the offending students was the son of another staff member. A few of the adults advocated for the students and asked that we let them stay at the camp. Nevertheless, I believed that I had no choice but to follow through with the policy that was in place—a policy to which the students and parents had both agreed. For me, this was a matter of integrity.

> While the rules had been clearly established, I never expected that I would actually have to fly anyone home—and I'll admit, I resented being put into the situation.

Proverbs teaches that the person who seeks godly wisdom will receive it, and will be discerning, acting in justice and fairness. It would have been easy to justify "giving in" as a wise decision. However, Proverbs 25:26 says, *Sometimes a godly person gives in to those who are evil. Then he becomes like a muddy spring of water or a polluted well* (NIrV.) I did not see giving in as a choice, or my authority and trustworthiness as a leader would forever be compromised.

I called the airlines and explained the situation. They were very helpful and volunteered to place a note in their files stating that they were minors who were being sent home from a camp for consuming alcohol. They were not to be allowed to sit together on the plane under any circumstances. The worship leader drove them into Denver to the airport, which gave him an opportunity to talk with them—a teachable moment. Unfortunately, they weren't in any mood to talk.

Though all of the parents had signed a form agreeing to pay for an airline ticket if their child violated the zero-tolerance policy and had to be flown home, none of the parents ever reimbursed the church. One of the students continued to participate in the youth ministry sporadically. Two of them were seniors at the time, and went on to college only a couple of months later. I attempted to reach out to them after the camp, but with little success.

An unexpected but welcomed outcome occurred during the camp itself. Two of the seniors, who had never quite accepted me as a "replacement" for their former youth minister, approached me one evening after the offending students had been sent home. They expressed their respect for me as a leader. They affirmed me for actually following through with the stated policy. One of them even sent me a letter later that summer, reiterating his thoughts. This strengthened my belief about the importance for a leader to act with integrity.

IN RETROSPECT

As time has passed, I have continued to reflect upon that camp experience. Sometimes I am haunted by "what ifs?" and wonder if I did the right thing. I do believe that I acted correctly, given the policy I had instituted, but I question the actual policy itself.

I was trying to preempt any drinking or other drug use by letting the students know that this would not be a "grace" situation. This was partly because I knew we would be involved in outdoor activities that would present them with a greater risk if they were using any type of drugs. But I really didn't expect anyone to be so bold as to violate the policy. Besides, the vast majority of my students were really good kids who would never even dream of using drugs or alcohol, let alone at a church event.

If I had it to do over again, I probably would have included the policy with language more like the following: *Any student using alcohol or other illegal drugs may be sent home at their parents' expense.* Simply changing the "will" to "may" provides some leeway for the leader to make the decision on the fly.

I have lost touch with those students over the years, as I now reside in another state. Perhaps I will be able to reconnect with them one day, which may help me to know how that decision has impacted their spiritual lives.

QUESTIONS TO CONSIDER

When is the last time I took a look through all of our youth ministry—and church-wide—policies? Will I be okay with enforcing them all exactly as they are written when the time comes?

In what situations do policies need to have some leeway for the leader to account for situational context? In what situations should policies be black and white in order to protect the leader from having to make certain decisions?

When policies are enforced that carry disciplinary consequences for offenders, what follow-up processes need to occur for the offenders, their families, and others in the group, so that ministry continues to be offered to everyone?

IT'S UNDER WATER
YOUTH TALKS GONE WRONG

Matt Laidlaw is the Program and Content Pastor of Anthem, the High School and Post-High School ministry at Mars Hill Bible Church in Grand Rapids, Michigan. He has served in student ministries as a volunteer, resident, and pastor for the past eight years. He's also lived and studied in the Middle East and is passionate about providing high school and college students the opportunity to experience the Bible and it's world through pilgrimage, teachings, and resources.

In order to generate some enthusiasm around teaching the Prophets of the Old Testament to our high school students, we began our Wednesday evening together with a game we titled "Jonah's Revenge." One student from each grade was invited to join us on stage, where we had four giant plastic tubs filled with gallons of water. The plastic tubs were clear, so that everyone in the audience could see the countless number of sardines that had settled to the bottom of each tub. The object of the game was for each contestant to retrieve as many sardines as possible from the bottom of the water-filled tub using only his mouth. The person who collected the most sardines would exact the most revenge on Jonah's behalf and would be declared the winner. Brilliant game, right?

Almost immediately after the game began, I noticed from my vantage point in the back of the room that a considerable amount of water was flying out of each tub as our four contestants dove for mouthfuls of sardines. I ran on stage and politely instructed all of our contestants to be "a little less violent" as they dove, because they were spilling too much water. Almost immediately after returning to my place in the back of the room, our sophomore contestant (who is exceedingly large and strong for his age) decided to stand-up, lift his plastic tub over his head, and dump out all of the water because, logically, diving for sardines would be much easier if there was no water left in the tub. Now, however, gallons of standing water covered our stage, guitars, microphones, drum kit, and keyboard! All instrument cables, extension cords, and plugs were completely submerged.

All at once I was confronted with the reality that my students on stage were in immediate danger of electrocution, that thousands of dollars of band and tech equipment could be damaged or destroyed, and that we still had nearly 90 minutes of programming ahead of us.

INEVITABILITY

Most youth ministry mishaps will be preventable based on your experience and intelligence, the nature of your students and programming, and of course, the grace of God. But nothing is foolproof, so we must make sure we're as prepared as possible. We need to accept the fact that there will be metaphorical floods that come our way. And we need to be ready to bail water during any potential situation in which our volunteers and students find themselves.

PREPARATION

In order to minimize risk (and in youth ministry there is always some risk), ensure that you are prepared by doing the following:

Plan Ahead. Outline basic policies and procedures for your students and volunteers to follow in case of severe weather, fires, security threats, or health related emergencies. Have other ministries and leaders in your community check your information to make sure nothing is missing and to confirm that everything you've outlined is consistent with other church policies. Compiling this information in a manual or training document with several hard copies located around the space where you most frequently gather with your students and volunteers isn't a bad idea.

Share the information. Being prepared means that you shouldn't be the only one who knows what to do if things get crazy. Hopefully you've already discovered that whether your ministry has 10 students or 300, you need to share your leadership responsibilities with eager interns, trusted volunteers, helpful parents, and high-capacity student leaders. Requiring training on the information outlined above (and hopefully much more) and sharing leadership responsibilities with other invested individuals ensures that you're not the only one responsible for making things right and you're not the only one who has something to lose when disaster strikes. When our stage flooded that evening, the three volunteers in our tech booth helped save day—not only because they were empowered to act through trust and our trainings but also because they had a personal investment in caring for the submerged equipment. Because our adult volunteers share ownership of our ministry, they shared ownership of cleaning up our mess.

> Because our adult volunteers share ownership of our ministry, they shared ownership of cleaning up our mess.

Expect the worst (and know what to do). Members of our ministry team roll their eyes whenever I say, "How might someone die if we decide to do this?" during our planning meetings. It sounds like an extreme and gruesome question, but after "Jonah's Revenge," a competition between our high school students that involved crowd surfing the most junior high students from point A to point B, and a watermelon eating contest that ended with a female freshman student's face covered in blood, I've learned the hard way that doing the work of asking critical questions about safety might save the life of a student or volunteer I love—along with saving my job. If we'd asked these kinds of questions as we planned "Jonah's Revenge," we likely would have decided against it. Just to be clear, asking these questions doesn't automatically eliminate ideas. It might just provide you with the safest possible version of your idea. We will have a watermelon-eating contest again this year, but we'll definitely enforce a rule against using your head as a hammer to smash the watermelon. (Because sometimes the watermelon moves and a kid ends up using his head to hammer the picnic table.) We'll also have a fully stocked first-aid kit close by.

> Members of our ministry team roll their eyes whenever I say, "How might someone die if we decide to do this?" during our planning meetings.

PROTECTING PEOPLE AND PROPERTY

The parents of your students and the families of your volunteers have extended you the trust of providing for the safety and care of the people they love most in the world. You and your team must take this sacred trust seriously and act urgently to protect the physical safety of everyone present once you realize there is a flood. Thus, plans for your program, or the disappointment of your students and volunteers cannot take priority over what will actually provide protection.

After our stage was drenched, the game was ended immediately and all of our students and volunteers were removed from the stage until we could turn off the electricity to that area of the room and clean up the water. Much to the dismay of our student band, we chose to postpone the next portion of our evening until we could guarantee everyone's safety.

Your community also trusts you to steward and care for your church's resources. You and your team must take this seriously and act urgently to protect church property and equipment once you realize there is a flood. Minimizing the fiscal cost the church might incur because of the disaster will

84 IT HAPPENS

help minimize consequences you might face with your boss or other church leaders. You won't be able to prevent all of the damage, but you can't let your desire to keep your program or event moving cost your church more money.

If you can't demonstrate responsibility with what you've already been given, you likely won't be trusted with more resources in the future. This will be a problem when it's time to submit next year's budget proposal to your leaders. We refused to turn our stage's power back on until we could guarantee that it wouldn't come at the cost of the church's or our volunteers' band equipment. This was a short-term disappointment but a wise decision in the long run.

ACKNOWLEDGING THE FLOOD WITHOUT DRYING OUT THE PROGRAM

Everyone who is present at your program or event will be fully aware of how disastrous the flood really is. In the chaos of the moment you might convince yourself that you can somehow hide the severity of the situation. This is a lie. Trying to gloss over the mess you've found yourself in will only cause you to lose credibility with your students and volunteers.

> Trying to gloss over the mess you've found yourself in will only cause you to lose credibility with your students and volunteers.

Once you've ensured the safety of the people and property that have been threatened by the disaster and you've decided not to send everyone home, you have to trust yourself enough to move forward with confidence. Acknowledge the reality of the flood and calmly direct your students and volunteers in a positive and productive direction with an alternative way forward. If you're constantly pointing students and volunteers to what went wrong earlier in your program or event you'll be giving them permission to dwell on the flood and not move forward with you.

In our situation with the drenched stage: we made the quick decision to eliminate a portion of our program; I made fun of how short-sighted our game was and how they might have a new high school pastor next week; I gave my talk on Jonah without a microphone and in more of a discussion format; and we dismissed students to their small groups earlier than normal. The night didn't go as planned, but it still served a purpose in spite of our unexpected disaster.

WE'VE ALL FELT LIKE WE WERE DROWNING

You need to go to bed every night knowing you're as prepared as possible so that you'll be able to sleep well on the night things go horribly wrong. When there is a flood in your ministry remember that you're not alone and that all of us have encountered a disaster of some kind. During the drive home on the evening we drenched our stage I couldn't help but tremble at the thought of how much worse things could have turned out, who could have gotten hurt, and how irresponsible I was. These kinds of thoughts quickly lead us to question our calling and ability to serve as pastors.

During floods you will likely be your greatest critic. Forgive yourself, and remember that our students and volunteers are more forgiving than we generally give them credit for. My students like to remind my team and me about "Jonah's Revenge" and the chaos of our waterlogged stage. When they do this, they remind me why I love my job and why it's so important to take it seriously.

QUESTIONS TO CONSIDER

How "bought in" are the adult volunteers to our ministry programs? If disaster struck, would they take the initiative to bail it out?

In what ways could we mitigate potential damages from unexpected floods with a little preplanning?

In what ways do we allow fears of unexpected disasters to inhibit creative events?

Beyond "people" and "property," are there other things we need to protect from potential disasters in our ministries?

STRANDED
FIGURING IT OUT ON THE FLY

Amy Jacober, when not busy teaching youth ministry courses and grading papers, loves playing with her two beautiful daughters and beating her husband at Ticket to Ride! She is a thriving survivor of more than 20 years of youth ministry, recently wrote *The Adolescent Journey*, and enjoys her family pet, a black boxer bigger than Clifford.

A carload of junior high girls stranded on the deck of a bar hoping for a place other than my car to sleep for the night. Not my finest moment in ministry, and certainly not one I had prepared for in any class or workshop.

I loaded up my car with the girls, and we headed out in plenty of time to make the snowboarding retreat. I was supposed to be the weekend speaker and had been working all month crafting the talks and times together. I had worked with the other two churches we would work with and was excited not only to be up in the snow but also to get to join with some other amazing people. I was even more excited to be a part of what I was certain was going to be a life-changing weekend in the lives of these girls.

Everything was perfect: directions in hand, car loaded, snacks aplenty, and we were off. The entire drive should have been no more than three hours. Sure, I had heard the weather reports that snow was on the way, but every forecast assured me (and the parents) that we would arrive safely and in plenty of time before the storm hit. So much for forecasts.

On the way up the mountain there were signs. Literally, I mean there were signs saying, "Buy your chains ahead." This seemed promising, and I thought nothing of just grabbing a set of chains for my car and knew I could get them on in short order. What I didn't know is that these signs had been out all day and actually referred to a store well up the mountain.

We inched our way there and were greeted by a friendly, laid back worker who let me know that the store actually had two separate sections. His was the section with skis; the section with chains closed for the night because of the storm. I did point out that all the signs were still out. "Yeah…we didn't want to go out into the storm. The store will be open in the morning."

The storm had moved in; we were still 50 miles from where we needed to be and these roads were ungroomed. With no chains, I could go no further, and I couldn't make it back down the mountain. We were stuck.

DILEMMA

The girls were hungry and cold, but we talked excitedly of the adventure we

90   IT HAPPENS

> Unfortunately, all the restaurants in town had shut down early because of the storm. Worse, every single hotel room in town was booked. Okay...don't panic.

were about to have. No problem. I knew how to book a hotel room and had a credit card in hand for just such emergencies. Unfortunately, all the restaurants in town had shut down early because of the storm. Worse, every single hotel room in town was booked. Okay...don't panic.

Next to the closed shop where I was supposed to be buying chains was a deck with people sitting outside and looking warm. It was the deck of a bar and had outside heaters. "Ladies, let's head for the deck." I called my pastor (whose daughter was with me) to let him know what was going on, and he was incredibly supportive and encouraging. He later told me he was scared to death for us but wasn't about to tell me that. He happened to be with the parents of the other girls, so everyone was kept in the loop. A quick prayer over the phone, then we hung up so I could conserve the phone's battery.

MY RESPONSE

I must say that if I must be stranded in a snowstorm, these were the best girls in the world to be stranded with. They settled around a table laughing, talking, and playing games. We talked about God's provision, our friendships with each other, and the fact that this would make a fantastic story later. My call finally went through to the lodge where we were supposed to be meeting the other churches. They had come up the other side of the mountain and had no problems. I offered a *mea culpa*, talked them through an activity for the night, and said we'd be there as soon as we could in the morning.

Our options were looking slim. Several people came out to smoke only to be awkwardly chased off by junior high girls giggling. Finally, one very friendly and slightly tipsy woman came over to say hello. She had just passed a licensing exam and was celebrating. We told our story, she told us not to worry—that she knew something would work out—and she slipped back inside.

Next thing we knew, a sober man came to us and said he was her husband. She had told him our story, and they wanted to invite us to their place for the night. He offered his address and phone number to pass on to parents back home, assuring us they were nice people. I called our pastor, let him know the offer, and awaited his direction. As this was the only option, with full parent approval, we headed to the home of complete strangers.

STRANDED 91

I could not have found better lodging if I had planned it. We walked into a warm home. They had a large guest room already filled with four beds and plenty of space for pallets. The woman immediately put on a kettle to make hot chocolate, then pulled together a meal for us. We settled for the evening on a giant comfy couch watching movies and eating popcorn. They were kind and generous with little fanfare and no expectation of return.

Our conversation turned once again to God's provision in ways we could never imagine. Each girl knew not to talk to strangers, certainly not to go to their houses—yet here we were. Cared for, provided for, and—after eventually making it to the retreat—we reflected that this first night was the warmest, most comfortable night of sleep for the weekend. The call home to parents, letting them know where we had landed, was amazing. They had all been praying and said they already knew we would be in a safe warm place for the night—but they hadn't realized how effective their praying would be.

We joined the rest of the group the next day. Snowboarding was great because of all the snow. Back at the lodge, the others had their own adventures the night before, and we came together to share stories, to share life, and—most importantly—to share Jesus. What I had prepared for the entire month before paled in comparison to the movement of God in our little group over the previous 24 hours. Matthew 6:25 took on a whole new level of depth.

IN RETROSPECT

This experience reminded me once again that many of the most impactful conversations take place in unplanned moments: in the nooks and crannies between Sunday school, small groups, preaching, teaching, and other planned times. One of the dirty little secrets of youth ministry is that most of the lessons we prepare, plan, study, and execute flawlessly will be forgotten; but the messy instances stick with us. The foibles, mishaps, and, sadly, often the moments we recount as flat out disasters—these are what become the "remember when" stories. It's in these moments when we as leaders can choose to get mad or frustrated, or we can simply give in to the unfolding events. Our attitudes can deter-

> One of the dirty little secrets of youth ministry is that most of the lessons we prepare, plan, study, and execute flawlessly will be forgotten; but the messy instances stick with us. The foibles, mishaps, and, sadly, often the moments we recount as flat out disasters—these are what become the "remember when" stories.

mine the kids' interpretations of even the worst of scenarios.

It is not a youth ministry secret that profound ministry can take place when we pay attention to the movement of the Holy Spirit even in the most trying of settings. It is also easy to tell a story in hindsight as if it were the easiest choice in the world to find the positive and trust God. In this situation, I was cold and hungry just like the kids. And I was scared to death that something bad would happen to one or more of the girls. I was acutely aware that I was the responsible adult in the group and that how I seemed to be handling it would set the tone for everyone else.

On the outside, I was confident and talked of the stories we would have. On the inside, I was freaking out! I had to choose to live out the Scriptures that I taught my students about trusting God's provision. The support of parents back home made a huge difference, as well. The amazing girls I had with me made things a whole lot easier, too. And the presence of the Holy Spirit with us—that made all the difference.

QUESTIONS TO CONSIDER

When the plans fall apart—and they absolutely will sometimes, maybe even often—what are my natural inclinations, and how can I guard against responding with fear, anger, or inappropriate words and actions? How can I ensure that my attitude will set a positive, Christ-like tone for students?

What rules that govern normal expected behavior (like, "Don't talk to strangers") are worth breaking at just the right times? What are the down sides of such decisions? Who all needs to be involved in those decisions?

Imagine being in a similar situation as these girls but being unable to reach parents or supervisors. How might that change the decision-making dynamics? What about if you can reach them but no consensus exists between pastor and parents?

LESSON DERAILED
GOSSIP ABOUT THE LEADER

Drew Smith lives and works in Tennessee. He misplaced his sanity sometime ago and has been looking for it ever since. In the meantime, he works with kids, where the loss of sanity is helpful and often appreciated. He also thanks God for the invention of storytelling, which keeps him remotely rational. Contact Drew at arsmith04@gmail.com.

A few months into the job, our class had wandered onto the subject of drinking. And, not surprisingly, my kids were somewhat split on the idea.

"I don't see what the issue is as long as you're not hurting anyone," one boy said.

"Okay. Good point. But couldn't you say that about a lot of things, like smoking pot?" I offered.

After a moment of hesitation, the boy replied, "Yeah, but that's different."

"How so?" I asked.

I thought I knew what I was doing. After all, I had prepared myself for these discussions, imagined them playing out in my head. I thought I knew what arguments might pop up, so I had a bunch of great comebacks all planned out. I felt ready for the fight.

Then, out of nowhere, came a bunker buster bomb—one of those comments that left me stuttering from shellshock.

A girl near the back of the class said, "I know who your *first* was."

For a brief moment, I thought I heard God laughing. Maybe this was a cosmic joke. Really? I knew I had to respond, but what could I possibly say to smooth something like that over? It would be like trying to clean up after an atomic bomb: it would take centuries, but before I could finish, I would die from the poisonous after-effects. In the confusion, I thought maybe I misunderstood the question.

With full stupidity, I asked, "My first what?"

Wow. Did I really just ask that question? Way to run screaming into oncoming traffic.

The girl laughed. "You know, your first. Do you remember Harmony?"

"Yes," I said. I recognized the name: a girl with whom I had attended high school.

"She told me that you were at a party and were drunk," the girl continued.

Oh, well, at least the story got better.

"She said you were her first," the girl concluded glibly.

Well, that was a good time. Truly a highlight of my career.

95

THE DILEMMAS

Thankfully, the story was an out and out lie. But I still had to figure out how to deal with it. I had a few options.

Investigate

I could attempt to root it out, find the person who started it, and squelch it at the source. But I really didn't want to "Sherlock Holmes" the winding trail of some stupid rumor. That could take days; and, to be frank, I didn't really care enough. But if the fount of the rumors was like Jesus' grace—never-ending and free for all—then it probably needed to be rooted out. With only one rumor in front of me, though, such a search might end up like a witch hunt.

Defend

I could call a meeting with everyone I knew and try to explain that any such rumor they may or may not have heard was completely false. But there's an old saying: *Stirring the poo makes it stink worse.* Since some people probably hadn't heard the rumor, bringing it up to them would have been like jumping into a whole river of poo. I may have smelt bad to my kids at that moment, but I didn't need everyone else to get whiff of that stench, too.

> Stirring the poo makes it stink worse. Since some people probably hadn't heard the rumor, bringing it up to them would have been like jumping into a whole river of poo.

Ignore

I could ignore it, but then I ran risk of it festering and growing into something altogether different. Some rumors are like cancer: They grow without any sort of intervention. Leaving it alone, then, could have resulted in the death of my career. Plus, I could've lost the respect of my kids if I didn't respond; and with the loss of respect, I could've lost my effectiveness with them.

Redirect

I could've also redirected the conversation back to the issue at hand. But kids are some of the best politicians out there, knowing how to play the game of avoiding guilt. They could have spotted my weak political move from a mile away. Besides, the last thing I wanted was for my actions to look like a cover up. I would have gone down in the scandal of Rumor-Gate, all the way declaring, "I'm not a crook!"

Face

Then there's the option I chose: address it then and there. I had to put that thought to rest immediately. Besides, after a suggestion like that, would the kids have listened and thought about anything else I said that day, anyway?

MY RESPONSE

Finally, my wits came back to me. I replied, "Well. Hmm. Let me put it this way. I have never drunk any alcohol. Also, I'm waiting until I'm married to have sex. And I'm not married yet. I'll let you put two and two together."

"But Harmony said…I don't understand. So she lied about it?" the girl asked with some bewilderment.

"I guess she did," I answered.

"I believe you," the girl continued. "I don't know why you would lie about being a virgin."

Oh, great, another topic to discuss.

"Well, the Bible says to wait, doesn't it?" one of the boys responded. The other guys nodded their heads in agreement.

Well, at least there was that silver lining.

IN RETROSPECT

While the terror of this experience passed quickly, it did provide me a point of reference for any future rumors that might rear their ugly heads.

Rumors can create serious issues for those of us who work with kids—especially the wrong kinds of rumors. Thankfully, while not without some potential damages, this rumor was dealt with relatively easily. The kids responded well to my answer, and it was never mentioned again. But how we deal with rumors will depend on the situation. Most rumors will go away on their own, but a few could potentially create great difficulties for us since we work with young people and are held to a higher standard. In such cases, it will most often be best to discuss the issue with our staff supervisor and key lay leadership. Even if it's not serious enough to cause us to lose our jobs, we still need to let our kids know the truth, as they're the ones who will be impacted by such rumors the most.

In light of such events, we should also stress the severity of rumors and the damage they can cause. In his letter to the Romans, Paul includes gossipers in with "God-haters" (1:30). Clearly God wanted Paul to tell people that gossip is something that can cause great pain; when we gossip, we are hurting one of God's children by spreading character-damaging stories that may or may not be true. And such talk is antithetical to the nature of God.

The writer of Proverbs says, "A soothing tongue is a tree of life, but perversion in it crushes the spirit" (15:4). In the creation story, the Tree of Life

> **Rumors are bullets of the tongue—and once they escape, they can ricochet from ear to ear until great damage is done.**

provided immortality, longevity. Similarly, our tongues can either bestow a healthy spiritual life or destroy it. Rumors are bullets of the tongue—and once they escape, they can ricochet from ear to ear until great damage is done. Some rumors are even powerful enough to forever damage someone's faith, regardless of their truthfulness. Our kids must understand this, and it probably wouldn't hurt for some of our adults to learn this lesson, either.

That takes care of *false* rumors. But what about those pesky true ones? No doubt there are some Facebook pictures that we all wish didn't exist. But in such instances, how do we respond? James said, "Confess your sins to each other and pray for each other so you may be healed" (James 5:26). We could try to lie about such rumors, but what good would that do? Our kids need to know we are not pillars of perfection, but, rather, men and women of imperfection struggling after the path created by our Savior. After all, God's great champions in the Bible were all sinners, too. Paul killed Christians. Noah got drunk. David committed adultery. Moses took credit for God's work. Peter denied Christ. These great leaders of faith were also sinners. God included these examples in the Bible to show that even otherwise godly people aren't perfect, but it was their faith that truly made them great. I may be ashamed of my past, but it is Christ in whom I place my pride and have hope.

In the end, when confronted with a rumor, we have to keep our cool. Then, according to the situation, we must deal with it appropriately, lest we provide more material for even more rumors.

QUESTIONS TO CONSIDER

What rumors have I heard lately, and how did I respond?

In what ways do I allow rumors to ricochet off my own ears and lips?

Gossip is so much a part of kids' lives that they often don't notice their participation. How can I intentionally create an environment where their gossip filters get strengthened?

How can I prepare myself for inevitable gossip about me so that I not only nip it in the bud but also create a teachable moment?

SNOWED IN
SEVERE WEATHER AND QUICKLY CHANGING PLANS

Oeland Camp has been serving in youth ministry full-time since 1992. He has been invited to be a keynoter, seminar speaker, and worship leader at various events; he has helped to develop local youth ministry networks in Alabama and South Carolina; and he has been on church staff with St. Paul's Summerville since 1998, where the Summerville Youth Network tries to reach students in the local community regardless of denominational boundaries.

Almost every youth minister has led a trip that turned into a nightmare. During my second year of ministry, I experienced my worst youth trip...so far, anyway.

I was an intern for a growing youth ministry in a beach community just a mile from the ocean. We had 42 kids in three vans and two trailers on a ski trip with a chase car following, and a great time seemed to be on the horizon. Then, everything fell apart. At a rest stop, one kid revved the engine in one van, slipped it into drive, and dropped the axle on the ground. Kids moaned through a two-hour delay to get it to the shop, while no other 15-passenger rental vans could be found. So, we just piled everyone on top of everyone else, without seatbelts, and continued into the mountains.

Then the blizzard set in.

Facing three days of relentless snow, we spent hundreds of dollars on tire chains that we would never use again. The temperature dropped to what felt like sub-zero weather, and our sun-tanned kids refused to go out on the ski slopes. Great ski trip.

The day we were going to leave, we loaded the trailers; and as we moved the van, the rubber tires actually ripped and remained frozen in the ice. The trailer pulled away, but bottoms of the torn tires were stuck in the parking spot. And, of course, the local U-Haul store was closed. My boss went into town to figure something out as I hauled the entire load of luggage into the ski lodge and waited.

Our stuff was spread everywhere in the lodge as kids whined. *Can I call my mom to come get me? I have a credit card; can I book a plane ticket?* Other customers complained. Management was angry. But what could I do? Out of personal desperation, I pulled out my acoustic guitar and started to distract myself. My group perked up, "Hey, Oeland, play us a song!"

No way.

But they persisted. The only song I could think of was "Awesome God" by Rich Mullins. So we started singing quietly (I eyed the manager hoping he wouldn't grab my guitar and smash it). And then...cue the majestic movie music...I heard more singing. More and more voices joined in, at first from

101

102 IT HAPPENS

my youth group, and then from others. Dozens of people from other tables, and even on the stairs, were singing along! I was amazed as groups of people started calling down requests from the balcony. I discovered that all those grumpy "customers" were actually other youth groups also stranded in the snowstorm.

Moments before we had been disgruntled, selfish, whiny individuals; now we were beginning to act like church.

IN RETROSPECT

I learned a lot of lessons through that experience that have helped me during subsequent activities when my plans don't go right.

Ask for the manager (ahead of time)

A little planning prevents pounds of pain. I now plan our meals by picking a food court in a mall or designated restaurant, and I call ahead. Managers love to make money, but they like hosting groups better if they know a few days ahead of time.

I also build in some memory makers by finding interesting local places to eat to bring the trip out of the "interstate" zone. I try to check with church members at my destination for discounts on hotels, rentals, and places to visit; and I am often surprised by who wants to help me host a successful trip. And if I find myself in a tight spot, it's a good idea to ask the manager for help. Often they can be very resourceful if they know why I suddenly brought forty kids into their store.

Planning pit stops helps all the drivers know where to go (pun intended). Before cell phones, we did this all the time; but in recent years we say, "I will call you when it is time to stop." Then we find out that someone's cell phone doesn't get coverage, and one van is in another state before lunch.

Plan for the unexpected

I find it annoying that a computer will say, "An unexpected error has occurred." *Of course* it is unexpected. What error is ever planned? But in youth ministry, we have to plan for errors. Flexibility is our friend.

Developing ways to compensate for possible delays in the scheduled trip can be useful.

For instance, the farther from home, the more I pad the cost per kid. Sometimes we just need to have an emergency stash of cash to turn a mountain into a molehill: snow chains, vehicle breakdowns, free ice cream as the tire gets changed, extra meals on the road, etc. Sometimes a little "grease" for the squeaky wheels makes the trip bearable instead of a complete bummer. Adaptability is key when things inevitably go wrong.

Work as a team

Giving away jobs to people who will do them with great passion magnifies our impact. Why should I carry all the money, find the restaurants, organized the rental vans, count the heads after every stop, set up rooming assignments, play "cop" during curfew hour, and lead all the devotionals? Handing out jobs creates shared authority and ministry. Jesus had a dozen disciples, yet many youth ministers try to survive on two volunteers.

The truth is that adults often want to help where there is a need, rather than watching one person run the show. Sharing lists of kids, maps of locations, phone numbers, and schedules allows other leaders to truly help us lead, not just chaperone. If I had brought a team of leaders during that snowstorm, I would not have had to carry the entire load of luggage by myself to the lodge, leaving me exhausted and moody.

> Adults often want to help where there is a need, rather than watching one person run the show.

Steer the van

In a crisis situation, we as leaders have an important tool to use to our advantage—our attitudes. One reason the group was having a miserable time was because *I* was having a miserable time. This is not insignificant. I could have done more to support my boss, the lead youth minister, rather than moping around about the luggage and the cold.

Colossians 3:1 encourages us to set our sights on Heaven, but I was only seeing the dirty snow and sour faces of the kids. In a poem titled "Attitude" by Charles Swindoll, I found a great insight: " I am convinced that life is 10% what happens to me and 90% how I react to it." As ministry leaders we need to realize that our attitudes steer the group in a particular direction.

If we only had a new church bus

It seems to be a common sentiment among smaller churches that all trips would be better if only we had a big church bus. We watch those giant, window-tinted monsters roll into the parking area with the church logo emblazoned on the side and feel envy—Christian envy, of course. More often, I get stuck with a caravan of mismatched rental cars, vans, and a few personal vehicles. In recent years, some state legislators and insurance agencies are rejecting the classic 15-passenger van design. Others celebrate their usefulness if driven safely, and many colleges, churches, and major rental carriers still use these large vans.

Several years ago, I was at a church that bought a 40-passenger bus. They had several reasons, but the youth ministry was a primary concern. I was excited initially about having a small army of drivers who would chauffeur me around so I could interact with kids instead of focusing on the road. But there are many hidden costs to owning such a large investment.

First, since the youth used it most often, it was my burden to keep it spotless at all times. I usually cleaned the bus once a week, and as far as I know, I was the only one to wash it off. Usually it was covered in leaves, sap, and dirt because it was parked under low hanging trees. Second, my volunteer pool dried up, so I had to get a CDL license myself. This resulted in another hidden cost: I no longer "needed" as many chaperones, so many of my volunteers stopped coming to trips. And finally, I discovered the yearly upkeep and repairs cost more than van rentals had in previous years.

Besides, once it broke down, the entire group was still stuck on the side of the road. A church bus can be a great blessing when the church embraces it as a ministry for the wider congregation. But it can also be a curse, especially if seen as a new responsibility for the youth minister.

The holiness of traveling

Abraham walked most of his life; Moses traveled across the wilderness twice; David fled from King Saul; and Elisha traveled to a foreign land to avoid famine. Even Jesus walked the length of Israel teaching people. And yet, he still took time to have special retreats for prayer (Mark 1:35), to be with the apostles alone (Matthew 16:13), or to reveal his glory to a select few (Mark 9:2).

Trips put us in a place apart; we get away from distractions; , and we see new horizons in the world and our faith. Going on a (well planned) trip can be one of the best prescriptions for youth ministry health and group bonding. Given 36 hours or more away from the cell phone and Internet, many young people find that their prayers feel richer, their faith deeper, and their vision of God more personal. This is why trips are such a common part of our programming each year.

QUESTIONS TO CONSIDER

What provisions have I made to handle the "unexpected errors?"

What jobs am I delegating to other adults in shared leadership? What additional jobs can I delegate?

Is my attitude set correctly? How do I expect the group to react if things don't go according to plan?

Am I grateful for the means of travel at my disposal, or am I constantly pining about how much better it would be "if only…"?

Am I clear about the reason for the trip? What is the focus? How will this improve the youth ministry: fellowship, spiritual, team building, etc.? How will I try to make room for the Holy in this experience?

9-1-1
YOUTH TRIPS AND HOSPITAL VISITS

Kelly Soifer is Director of Recruiting and Leadership Development for the Free Methodist Church in Southern California. She was a youth pastor for 15 years, and before that, a regional director for Young Life. She teaches at Westmont College and a Christian high school and writes articles for *Youthworker Journal*, YMToday. com, Fuller Youth Institute, and *Light & Life Magazine*.

"It was the best of times, it was the worst of times..." Most Americans will recognize those words from the opening of Charles Dickens' *The Tale of Two Cities*, a classic in Western literature and required reading in most high schools. Though this novel profiles the social upheavals of 18th century France and England, this phrase also perfectly summarizes my history with summer camp as a youth worker!

My own best memories of meeting Christ in high school revolve around camp. From a crazy river-rafting weekend in the spring to a weeklong summer camp in the Sierras to working for five weeks at a camp in the Rockies, the foundations of my relationship with Jesus were anchored in Christian camping.

I must add, however, that going to camp as a counselor, and then as a Young Life area director and youth pastor, is an entirely different experience. This is a reality that took a little too long to sink in. It is embarrassing to admit this in print, but one of my motivations for going into vocational youth ministry was the naïve notion in my 23-year old brain that I would be *paid* to go to and work at camps as part of my job.

Camp is nearly the best place for a young person to have an encounter with God: getting away from the distractions of home and being surrounded by God's incredible creation does something amazing. I have seen it happen time and time again since 1982 when I started as a volunteer youth leader, and I cannot be convinced otherwise.

> Perfectly responsible students (and adults!) often cast aside their better judgment and do the stupidest things!

However, camp is also a time of reckless abandon. Perfectly responsible students (and adults!) often cast aside their better judgment and do the stupidest things! While much of the damage can be attributed to an adolescent lack of wisdom, part of the reason for these mishaps must rest squarely on the shoulders of the adults in charge.

Poorly conceived and downright *Jackass*-like games planned by immature and testosterone-laden recreation directors have been the downfall of my teenagers countless times. Many injuries, from getting knocked out by running full force into a tree, to broken bones from slip 'n slides, have been the order of the day. But the most instructive experience in my career resulted from an incident that occurred due to my greatest camp nemesis: The Night Game.

The details of this incident's game have long been forgotten in my mind. Perhaps that is because I never really comprehend the "rules" of these games in the first place. Regardless of the elaborate "strategy" that is created, it always feels like the game is a warmed-over version of Capture the Flag, with some crazed running and screaming in complete darkness thrown in.

During Night Games I tend to hide somewhere and count the minutes until the horn is blown and the game is called. During this infamous event, however, I heard my name being shouted by several voices, and I knew this meant only one thing: Someone from my group had gotten hurt. I scrambled out from my hiding place and ran to the snack bar, where my student, a girl named Andrea, had fallen in a patch of cactus. (Oddly, no one ever asked why we were playing a night game amidst patches of cactus in the first place.) Her wrist really hurt, but it didn't look swollen.

THE DILEMMA

The camp medic (a.k.a., someone trained in a short first aid course) was attempting to assess the damage. I knew Andrea well. She was not a drama queen. She looked like she was in a decent amount of pain but was trying to be a good soldier. There seemed to be a spot where a sliver or thorn might have gone in. Andrea told us that she couldn't squeeze her hand. The medic (I continue to use the term loosely) tried to squeeze out the sliver. Andrea teared up. I stepped in.

"Isn't there a trained medical staff member somewhere at this camp?" I asked.

"The nurse on duty is busy dealing with a broken bone at another part of the camp." (We had four different camps running simultaneously.)

"I would like a professional to look at her wrist," I insisted.

"My friend who is visiting for the weekend is in his first year of med school," the "medic" offered, optimistically.

I shrugged my shoulders. We took a golf cart down to main camp where the med student was staying. He tried a little more aggressively to get the sliver out. By now Andrea couldn't close her hand at all. I should mention that she played the piano phenomenally well, and I envisioned that skill going down the drain—and to be honest, me facing the unending wrath of her mother.

The camp staff suggested she take a couple of Advil, go to bed, and see how it felt in the morning. I weighed my own priorities—I was in charge of a group of 75 other campers and counselors. It was midnight on the second night of camp. I desperately wanted to go to bed myself. I envisioned staying up all night for what was potentially a sliver and a slight wrist sprain. What to do?

Despite the counsel from the camp staff, who faced these sorts of scenarios weekly, I made my decision based on a tried-and-true motto: *better safe than sorry.* I asked for the information on how to take Andrea to the closest emergency room, which was 25 minutes away. I called her parents, even though it was 1:00 a.m. by then, and I feared I would be upsetting them unnecessarily.

I wish I had the space to describe the hilarious and somewhat frightening scenario that unfolded that night. We arrived at an emergency room that was really busy and lined up behind three other cases: a drive-by shooting, a nervous breakdown and a drunk woman with an acrylic fingernail stuck in her ear canal. (I am not making this up.)

After waiting four hours, Andrea's wrist was x-rayed and it was discovered that she had a two-inch long thorn in her tendon! The ER doc attempted minor surgery on Andrea's wrist to remove the thorn, which nearly sent *me* to the emergency room as my stomach (and nerves) flip-flopped. It was decided, this time by trained medical professionals, that she needed to go home and have the thorn removed surgically.

It left a 1½-inch long scar on her wrist, and she kept playing the piano after having a cast on her arm for six weeks.

IN RETROSPECT

> My number one job as a youth leader is to be a young person's adult advocate, not his friend.

Fundamentally, the overarching point that I will never forget as a result of this experience: the kid in my youth group student is someone's child. My number one job as a youth leader is to be a young person's adult advocate, not his friend. Andrea's parents—and every parent of every student I have known since becoming a youth leader—had entrusted their sons and daughters to my care in allowing me to take them to camp. We all need to take that responsibility *very* seriously. My job was not to be cool and funny and to make sure she had an unforgettable spiritual high during her week at camp. My job was (and is) to be a responsible, godly adult and to do my best to guide every student in my care through an adventurous (yet safe) week.

Through far too many accidents (some of which were avoidable, many of which were not), I have learned a few simple principles:

1. **Always have medical forms for every trip that students must complete and parents or guardians sign ahead of time.** Most camps require these, but I have copied their format and used these for every overnight trip. I make sure they are completed thoroughly, and that I have up-to-date medications listed and working phone numbers for emergency contacts. It is well worth the extra effort. Though I may only need them once in my career, it could mean life or death. Seriously.

2. **Only listen to the judgment of trained medical professionals.** Most camps are not required by law to have doctors or nurses on the property at all times, and even fewer retreats, campouts, and mission trips require them. It is my job to get kids the care they need rather than pooling the collective ignorance (however well meaning it may be) of untrained students or adults on the trip.

3. **Give clear feedback to camps about their games and activities.** Sure, sometimes I feel like the fuddy-duddy, but I believe I have talked to camp directors after nearly every pool competition. Games that seem hilarious and fun in preparation are sometimes very dangerous in practice. Today I have no problem letting them know, "My kids didn't feel safe in that game," or "I nearly drowned as I was shagging balls in that water basketball game."

4. **Make sure other staff and adult volunteers understand basic safety routines and expectations:** I was once asked what is the top quality I look for in an intern, and my response was surprising to many: "Someone with a healthy fear of what could go wrong." I can teach leaders to lead Bible studies or counsel students at camp; but if they do not have an inherent understanding of their responsibilities as an adult role model and decision maker, I'm sunk.

QUESTIONS TO CONSIDER

When is the last time I have seriously pondered what could go wrong before a trip? What would change about my preparation if I thought about it a little more?

In what ways have I taken shortcuts with the "better safe than sorry" principle and later realized how fortunate I was that things turned out the way they did?

Are all of the leaders on my team in one accord regarding the way we would deal with emergency situations? If not, how can we get on the same page?

MISTAKE SNOWBALL
WHEN ONE BAD DECISION LEADS TO ANOTHER

Sara Bailey has been in youth ministry since 1993 serving Episcopal churches in North Carolina, Tennessee, and Pennsylvania. She is a ministry consultant and speaker in the Diocese of North Carolina, and she serves nationally as a lead consultant for Youth Ministry Architects. Sara lives in Greensboro with her husband, Geoff; their daughter, Madison; and their two dogs, Kyah and Sadie.

When I was at my second youth ministry job, I thought I knew it all. Here I was, this Southern gal who moved to the great, white Northeast where on my third day, the blizzard of the century (at least, that's what they called it on the news) came through blanketing my world with 30 inches of snow. This would mark the beginning of what I call my "learning" church experience.

That first year, a family in the congregation graciously offered their second home in Manchester, Vermont, as a place to stay for a youth group ski trip. I was a little skeptical that their home could house a large group of kids, let alone all the ski equipment that would come with us. Not one to turn down a gift, though, I accepted their offer without too many questions in the hopes that all would turn out okay.

Mistake #1: Not thoroughly checking out the accommodations.

Catherine (the teenage daughter) assured me there were enough beds for everyone, because they had a large family. This home, while beautiful, was older and had many of the characteristics of an old home: few bedrooms, small bathrooms, and a tiny kitchen. We ended up with rather sensitive plumbing issues, having to space out the water usage; for example: no showers while cooking in the kitchen, and two people couldn't flush the toilet at the same time. Fortunately there were no plumbing disasters that weekend. All of the girls ended up in a bed, though, and we had enough floor room for the guys. In the end, the house was a blessing, allowing for great fun, gathering, worshiping, eating, and snoozing.

Lesson learned, though: check out the accommodations more thoroughly next time.

The Friday night of our departure, it began to snow. My immediate instinct was to cancel the trip because it wasn't safe to drive in the snow. I was wrong and was quickly reminded that roads and highways are cleared much more quickly in the North than in the South where everything shuts down at the mere mention of snow. So we waited a few hours to let the heaviest snow pass

117

118   IT HAPPENS

through. Then we hit the road around 10 p.m. for our six-hour journey.

Mistake #2: Driving all night with very little sleep.

I can recall having a death grip on the steering wheel of one of the 15-passenger vans we had rented (back in the day when that was allowed). For the first few hours, it was still snowing and I was praying hard to avoid falling asleep or getting into an accident. My prayers were answered around the time we crossed the state line into New York: the snow stopped, and the Diet Coke kicked in.

Even though we arrived safely at our destination, it was four in the morning when we got there, and we had planned to hit the slopes at 8 a.m. Sleep deprivation, while common in youth ministry, is not a good thing for the person in charge. I never operated well on little sleep (and still don't). And I had started the trip already tired from all the preparation and running around at the last minute to be ready to take the group skiing. We adjusted the wake up time to leave the house at 10 a.m. Ugh!

> Sleep deprivation, while common in youth ministry, is not a good thing for the person in charge.

By the time I wound down from the all the Diet Coke I had drunk to stay awake, I got less than three hours of sleep. I can remember being irritable, cranky, and extremely bossy that day. Those who crossed my path in what might be perceived as a negative way got their heads bitten off. This was one of those times the group was led by "Psycho Sara" rather than "Sweet Sara." It was not my best moment. My hope is that the teens and adults will have forgiven me by now for being such a witch.

Lesson learned: Try, try, try hard to be well-rested before a youth trip; otherwise, poor leadership and decision-making reigns.

Mistake #3: No adult supervision.

The day went well at the slopes: perfect snow pack and relatively short ski lift lines. At the end of the day, we headed home for some grub and warm clothes. The teens were rejuvenated after a scrumptious spaghetti dinner, so Catherine suggested the group go sledding on a nearby hill. All of the youth bundled up and scooted out the door. It didn't even occur to me that an adult wasn't with the group. In my sleep-depleted, post-dinner haze, I didn't bother to ask Catherine exactly where they were going.

> All of the youth bundled up and scooted out the door. It didn't even occur to me that an adult wasn't with the group.

For about 20 minutes, there was peace and quiet in the house. Then, Catherine came crashing in the door frantically telling me that Jack had been hurt. I grabbed my coat and raced outside in search of Jack. We met him and the rest of the group about halfway between the sledding hill and the house. I took one look at Jack and knew he needed medical assistance. Jack had been at the bottom of the hill, still reeling from the ride down, when another teen named Ben came down the slope on an old-fashioned sled—the kind with metal rails they probably don't make anymore. Ben lost control of the sled, Jack couldn't get out of the way fast enough, and they collided. The metal rail had slammed into Jack's face leaving him with a broken nose and a gash that went from the middle of his left cheek, up the side of his nose, crossing over his nose up between his eyebrows, curving around the eyebrow and ending at that spot just between his eye and the bridge of his nose. It was the shape of jagged shepherd's crook.

Lesson learned: Having an adult present may not have prevented the accident from happening, but an adult could have assessed the injury quickly and managed the crisis. I found out later that the teens really didn't think it was that bad (it was dark, and there was only moonlight for illumination), so they took Jack to the nearest bathroom, which happened to be at the Equinox Hotel—a fancy, historic hotel that my youth group couldn't afford. Apparently they were there trying to stop the bleeding for a bit before they realized that Jack needed medical attention.

Mistake #4: Not having a first aid kit readily available and not knowing where the nearest medical facility was located.

We took Jack back to the house and tried to find adequate bandaging for the short-term. There wasn't much of anything since I didn't think to bring a first aid kit with us. So we grabbed a bunch of towels, jumped in the van, and Catherine directed us to the nearest medical facility that she knew of. It was closed. Many phone calls later, we finally discovered that we needed to drive an hour to reach the closest hospital. In the meantime, Jack was coherent, able to talk to his parents on the phone, and hanging in there on what seemed like the longest drive ever. In the end, he got treatment and left six hours later with 30+ stitches, a broken nose, a black eye, and a swollen face. To this day, I thank God that the injury wasn't worse. The doctor told us numerous times how lucky Jack was; he easily could have lost his eye.

Lesson learned: Be prepared for medical emergencies (or any emergency). Even with an adult present with the sledding group, the accident was probably not preventable. But we could have been better prepared and equipped to deal with it. Always take a first aid kit. Have properly filled out medical forms. Know where the nearest medical facility is located and if it's open 24 hours.

IN RETROSPECT

As I reflect back on this incident 15 years later, I see that the trip started with some small mistakes but ended with some big ones. I am thankful: that Jack wasn't hurt more seriously, that Jack's parents were very understanding and grateful for us taking care of their son, that all the parents trusted me and the adult leaders with the care of their children, and that we all made it home in one piece, albeit a little banged up.

I have now learned:

Seek…for answers to all my questions in preparing for any youth event.

Sleep…it is imperative to be well-rested in order to make sound decisions.

Supervision…always, always, have an adult (preferably two) present with the youth wherever they are.

Safety…above all; ensure the physical, emotional, psychological, and spiritual safety of the lives entrusted to me.

QUESTIONS TO CONSIDER

Thinking back through the basics, what could I do to be better prepared for some of the inevitable things that will happen on trips?

Have I done due diligence concerning all aspects of the trip, including site visits where possible, prior to the group's arrival?

In what ways can I mitigate damages from unexpected problems that will crop up so they don't build up momentum in a mistake snowball?

SECTION 2:
DEALING
WITH ADULTS

DISGRUNTLED
THE ANGER-RIDDEN PARENT

Jim Hampton is professor of youth ministry at Asbury Theological Seminary. Prior to becoming a professor, he served as a local church youth pastor, a denominational leader, and co-founder of Barefoot Ministries, a youth ministry publishing company. He and his beautiful wife, Carolyn, have two great kids—Alyssa and Nathan—who are his primary youth ministry. Jim is a lifelong Cincinnati Reds fan, but don't hold that against him.

My senior pastor's words stung. "Jim, I think you should start looking for another position."

The issue revolved around the parents of a high school girl. The mom and stepdad were faithful church members, involved in leadership positions at the church and in the community. The daughter had been really attached to the previous youth pastor. While the girl was also involved in church, she was also involved in other activities that her parents knew nothing about.

We had a lake near our church where kids from town would often gather on the weekends to party. This often involved copious amounts of booze, marijuana, and sexual escapades. As a youth pastor in the area, I knew many of the kids who gathered there, and so when I showed up one Friday night, most of the kids who saw me simply waved, acknowledged me, and then continued their activities.

The one person who did not see me was this girl. I had seen her at a distance, walked up behind her, and called her by name. She turned around with a beer in one hand and a cigarette in the other, saw it was me, and froze. I asked her if we could talk privately for a moment, at which point I suggested she might want to leave. She agreed and actually let me drive her home.

> She turned around with a beer in one hand and a cigarette in the other, saw it was me, and froze.

Later, I heard from some other youth group members that she had been mortified at the experience—as much by the fact that I had caught her as the fact that she felt I had thoroughly embarrassed her in front of her friends (even though I had pulled her aside privately).

It was shortly thereafter that she started taking a decidedly unfriendly approach to me. She complained to her parents about having to go to youth group. She didn't want to attend Sunday school and only grudgingly came to worship. While I was aware of why this was happening, the parents were not. They assumed the issue was with me, so they decided to talk with the senior pastor about it. He then asked me to resolve the issue.

DILEMMAS

While I knew why the girl was acting this way, the question was how to talk about it with her parents in a way that would help us reach a satisfactory resolution. So I set up a lunch meeting with the stepdad, who had been the more vocal of the two about the situation, to discuss what was happening. I wanted to make sure that I was fully aware of his perspective before jumping to conclusions. Furthermore, I wanted to ensure I was approaching the issue from a biblically and theologically guided response rather than an emotional one.

I knew myself well enough to recognize that when others blame me, I can become defensive pretty quickly. So by sticking to the issues, and resolving to approach this theologically, I knew I would fare far better than if I got pulled into an emotional blame game.

As the stepdad and I talked, it quickly became evident that neither he nor his wife were aware of any of the extracurricular activities in which she was participating. I carefully broached these with the stepdad, suggesting that her reactions may have more to do with my catching her engaged in these things than in my ability to minister to her. The stepdad became very defensive, putting the blame squarely on me and acquitting his stepdaughter. There was no way, he argued, that she could be involved in these things, as they were fully aware of all that she did.

As he talked, I quickly realized that this was a case where his own relationship with his stepdaughter was tenuous at best. His responses were an attempt to shift the blame—and the responsibility for the faith formation of this child—to me. It was my fault she wasn't coming to church and my fault she wasn't growing in the faith; therefore, he was going to ask the board to have me removed.

MY RESPONSE

I came to the realization that I was not going to help this parent see beyond his own pain and hurt in order to find a way forward for his daughter. The more we talked, I came to better understand his hurt—and his inadequate understanding of the importance of faith formation happening in both the home and the faith community. His basic premise was that I was the youth pastor; therefore, it was my fault if she didn't want to come to youth group. He

> He was content to put the full blame for her lack of faith formation on me as her youth pastor.

was content to put the full blame for her lack of faith formation on me as her youth pastor.

After returning to the church that afternoon, I talked at length with my senior pastor about the issue and the conversation I had with the stepdad. While my senior pastor was sympathetic, he also told me that it was my responsibility to work it out with the stepdad—and quickly.

Further meetings were scheduled. I apologized and took responsibility for the areas in which I knew I could have done better. But I also suggested (pastorally, of course) that there were areas for which he and his wife could also take more responsibility, primarily in the role of parents serving as the primary spiritual caregivers (as opposed to the youth pastor) for their daughter. We had what I believed were several productive talks over the course of several weeks, and I truly thought we had worked everything out.

So imagine my surprise when, a few weeks later, my senior pastor called me into his office and related to me the need to start looking, giving me eight weeks to find something. As I talked with my pastor, it became apparent that even though I had followed biblical and theological principles to guide our discussion and attempted to reach a mutual Christian resolution, the stepdad had already made up his mind and would not budge. And since he carried great weight with the church board, he was able to persuade them I had to go.

IN RETROSPECT

As I sat in my office later that afternoon, I kept wondering what I could have done differently. With the hindsight of 14 years, I think I can honestly say, "Nothing."

Through that particular episode in my life, I've come to realize that sometimes, even though we may do careful biblical and theological reflection on a situation, allowing that reflection to then inform our praxis, in the end we are still at the mercy of how sinful, fallible people (of which I am one) respond. And unfortunately, not everyone we encounter will be open to the persuasion of the full gospel in his or her life. Even when we follow the right steps, we sometimes won't end up with the results we desire.

Years later, I have a more nuanced understanding of working with disgruntled parents. I recognize that I will never be able to appease all of them, no matter what I do. Instead, I choose to continue to do the same type of theologically informed praxis I did back then. Fortunately, most often, conflicts are successfully resolved. However, sometimes they are not, and those are painful moments. Regardless of what the outcome may be, in the end I have to realize that I can only control my actions and my response as I attempt to faithfully represent the gospel.

I've heard several colleagues say, "Careful theological reflection should always lead to faithful practice." I've come to believe that an addendum should be added, to that: "Careful theological reflection should always lead to faithful practice—but sometimes you'll still bleed."

QUESTIONS TO CONSIDER

As Christ-followers, we should try our best to keep from provoking others to anger. What are ways in which I exacerbate the anger of others, and how can I do less of that?

Even when I do everything right, some will still get angry with me. How should I respond to that?

Since fear should not be a primary motivator in my personal or professional life, where are the conversations or situations I've been avoiding simply out of fear of others' anger that need my attention in order to be a faithful youth minister?

HIGH-MAINTENANCE
THE HELICOPTER PARENT

Steve Argue is the life development director at Mars Hill Church in Grand Rapids, Michigan. He has been involved in youth ministry for the past 17 years as a youth pastor, instructor, speaker, consultant, and writer. In addition to his role at Mars Hill, he teaches seminary courses on youth ministry and is a doctoral student at Michigan State University, studying emerging adulthood, teaching and learning, and spirituality. More about Steve at marshill.org.

Bill and Jane were every youth worker's dream. They registered their daughter, Sarah, for the freshman camp *before* the deadline. They actually came to the parent meetings. Eventually they started volunteering as small group leaders, filling the empty spots I had hoped and prayed for. As the year progressed, Bill and Jane proved to be faithful volunteers who showed up consistently, prepared diligently for their freshman small groups, and even recruited another couple to be volunteers.

Come December, I had my winter retreat all planned. Some of the church's college students were back from break and, based on their history with the church and their winter break availability, I arranged for them to be leaders for the winter retreat. Due to limited space and budget, I emailed Bill and Jane to let them know I did not need them to be leaders on the trip, though they had volunteered to go. A day after I sent the email, Jane called. She explained that she and Bill had hoped to go on the retreat to be with Sarah. They explained that they believed in doing things as a family and wanted to experience the winter retreat with Sarah, as well as serve the ministry. I thanked Jane for her enthusiasm, but told her that I had already contacted leaders and that I was all set. Jane said that she understood, but that she and Bill were "very disappointed."

I'm not sure exactly when it hit me, but I noticed Jane and Bill's small comments and feedback seemed to grow with more intensity over the second semester. Just after the retreat, Jane called asking why the conversation of sex came up in Sarah's cabin and wanted to know the cabin leader's position on "how far was too far." Bill was more vocal each week about the boys getting "out of control." I could count on emails showing up in my inbox after each youth talk offering "friendly feedback" about my performance based on whether Sarah "liked it" or "got anything out of evening."

By spring, I was reviewing student applications for the mission trip I was taking that summer. Typically this trip was reserved for upper classmen, but the last few years, I did take upcoming sophomores, if there was space and if I felt the student was ready. In front of me was Sarah's application. Sarah was a good kid, but I could tell that her parents heavily orchestrated her involvement in youth group. I knew enough of Sarah to know that she wasn't ready for the trip and chose another underclassman for the remaining spot. After the communication went out to those accepted and those not, I received an email from Jane, asking to have a meeting with me immediately.

The next day I met with Bill and Jane. They were very upset that Sarah did not get picked for the mission team explaining that Sarah was likely more mature than most the students going on the trip. Further, they explained that Sarah had to go on a mission trip this summer, as the next summer would be filled with visiting colleges. While I empathized with Bill and Jane, they were not willing let the issue rest. Bill reminded me that they have been faithful members of this church for more than five years. They had served in my ministry and were consistent financial contributors to the church. Further, Bill reminded me that he was friends with most of the people on the elder board, and if Sarah did not go, they felt like they would have to "pass along their concerns."

> Bill reminded me that he was friends with most of the people on the elder board, and if Sarah did not go, they felt like they would have to "pass along their concerns."

Surprised by where this was going, I told Bill and Jane that I'd have to think about it. "Thank you," they said. "Think and pray about it. I'm sure you'll know what to do." They left. And I sat there stunned. What should I do?

WHAT HAPPENED?

The truth is that the above story has run its course more than once—in my ministry and in the youth ministries of many of my colleagues. Chances are, plenty of other youth ministers will run into a similar situation where, what initially seems like God's answer to your ministry needs, or hope that you're making progress in connecting with parents, takes a wrong turn along the way. Since youth ministry is an intentional effort to enter the lives of adolescents and their families, youth ministers experience the opportunities and risks of entering into the family dynamic—experiencing the good, the bad, and the ugly. In this case, something goes wrong. How can eager, giving parents who desire to be involved in their child's life become people who are challenging your ministry?

In these cases, there have been times where I, and other youth ministers I have worked with, have bowed to the pressure, while other times I/we have fought it. The stakes can get rather high as the choices we make with parents often affect our ministry philosophy. Some youth ministers end up bowing to parental, political pressure. Others distance themselves from parents. Both are unhealthy and can affect one's ministry trajectory, and it has made me realize that there are parental dynamics and warning signs that youth ministers much catch early on.

> Some youth ministers end up bowing to parental, political pressure. Others distance themselves from parents. Both are unhealthy and can affect one's ministry trajectory.

REFLECTING FURTHER

The term "helicopter parent" has often been used to define parents like Bill and Jane. Helicopter parents have been defined as "always hovering, ultra-protective, unwilling to let go, and enlisting 'the team' (parent, physician, lawyer, other counselors) to assert a variety of special needs and interests" (Howe & Strauss, *Millennials Go to College*, 2007). Part of enlisting "the team" includes the youth minister in ensuring that a parent's child is set up to succeed in every aspect of life, including his spiritual life. While there are usually negative connotations associated with overly involved parents, let's take a step back and reflect on this phenomenon from a few angles in order to appreciate the parental dilemma and the important role youth ministers play.

1. We live in a competitive and threatening world.

In our western culture we have witnessed the escalating pressures and fears associated with adolescents growing up in our society. More expectation is placed on them to "make it" in society, and increasingly more fear stems from the increase of global and school violence. Youth ministers should remember that these factors place a tremendous amount of stress on adolescents and their parents, often causing parents to pay closer attention to their children's success and safety.

2. We live in a society where few advocate for adolescents.

Further, parents are finding that few advocate for their own children. If parents do not address educational, social, and health issues, the systems currently in place will often fail to respond to the particular needs of their kids.

Parents often feel alone in their desire to help their child grow into adulthood. Their tactics, while coming off as strong at times, often are attempts to stem the tide of society that does not share support for their child with them.

3. We have youth ministries that need parents, volunteers, and sometimes, parent-volunteers.

For youth ministry to truly be effective, youth ministries need parental support, connection, and investment. Failure to appreciate this dynamic fails to see the broader context of which a student is part. Youth ministers often do not take into consideration what it means to have parents involved. Lack of a clear vision for parents in your ministry will often result in two things: 1) the absence of parents in your ministry, or 2) parents playing roles that knowingly or unknowingly undermine your ministry.

Therefore, I offer a few parameters that I've developed through some trial and error:

- A diverse leadership is my goal. Inviting parents into my ministry ensures a more diverse, intergenerational approach that provides a variety of perspectives that can inform and clarify our ministry practices. The more diverse our leadership team, the better.
- Before inviting parents into volunteer roles, I like to ask them if they have received permission from their child. This may seem odd, but I have found it very valuable to ensure adolescents are comfortable with having their parents that close to one of their social domains. Remember that each adolescent is at a different place on his or her journey of differentiating (becoming independent) from parents. This conversation respects the young people and slows overzealous parents from forcing their way in. I recommend requiring this conversation with parent and teenager, and following up with your own conversation, as well.
- If parents get the green light from their teenager, I have had better results when I established clear boundaries about what it means to be a volunteer in your ministry. Parents must learn to wear their "volunteer hat" when they serve and not their "parent hat." When talking with parent-volunteers about certain topics, it doesn't hurt to ask the parent, "Which hat are you wearing right now—your parenting hat or your volunteer hat?" Keeping the boundaries clear helps avoid blurred lines of authority, power struggles, or favoritism.

- Revisiting the parent-volunteer experience after each ministry year allows me to address any issues that point toward role-confusion. I am convinced more than ever that keeping a confused parent-volunteer just because I need people to run the ministry is a bad idea.

4. We must have youth ministers who know how to pastor both adolescents and their parents.

Finally, we should remember that our volunteers and we are not merely ensuring the spiritual growth of our students. Volunteers and parents are being challenged by their own faith journeys, which means youth ministers must be committed to shepherding students *and* their parents during this period of life. This means courageously confronting some parents' unhealthy, helicopter tendencies. For others, it means asking them to be more involved. For all, it requires time and attention and provides a necessary voice to teenagers and parents who need to hear the good news that God is faithfully guiding them through the challenging yet exciting time of adolescence.

QUESTIONS TO CONSIDER

What are the primary recurring helicopter parent issues in my youth ministry currently? What are the principles that we are violating, and what are we upholding?

Who are the high-maintenance parents right now, and in what ways have my actions been unhelpful to the situation? What fences need mending soon?

Since parents are ultimately more accountable for their kids' spiritual development than I, how much of my frustration is about my own inconvenience, and how much is truly related to stifling the spiritual growth of their kids?

Since God is ultimately interested in reconciliation for all, how can I "speak the truth in love" in ways that do not alienate but rather build bridges?

SMUG
THE SMARTER-THAN-YOU PARENT

Len Evans is a youth ministry activist who oversees Texas and New Mexico for the National Network of Youth Ministries, serves on the advisory board for We Love Our Youth Worker US, and is the Pastor of Simply Soul Care, a free pastoral care service for youth workers. He has written about youth ministry for more than ten years and is a regular contributor to *Group* Magazine.

I had been at my first church for only a few months when I encountered something that had never been addressed in any youth ministry class I'd taken or textbook I'd read. A few parents would occasionally keep their kids home during our midweek meeting so they could do homework. Our church was in the back yard of an Ivy League University, and the level of academic intensity was unlike anything I had seen before. A good number of our students went on to different Ivy League schools; and for many of them, Duke was actually their "safety school."

To me, the idea of missing Bible study in order to increase an academic edge felt like spiritual immaturity. Of course, I never attended an Ivy League school, either, but I didn't feel like it made me stupid.

I shared my frustration with other youth ministers, because I didn't know if I was the only one experiencing that or if it was fairly common for the area. Parents weren't punishing their kids, but the staying home was a consequence of the kids having not finished their homework.

Honestly, I didn't fully get it until I kept my own daughter home from youth group when I was her youth pastor.

LOOKING FORWARD

In some ways, it was a joyous season of youth ministry when I was young, leading students who were not much older than I was. It's a lot easier to be the young, cool, cousin type of youth worker than it is being the older, much-less-cool, uncle type.

> It's a lot easier to be the young, cool, cousin type of youth worker than it is being the older, much-less-cool, uncle type.

As a young married couple, we didn't have children until we were two years into my first youth ministry position. The parents of teenagers saw me differently after I became a parent, because I was different. Some things cannot be fully understood from a book, a workshop, or through observations—

140 IT HAPPENS

things where experience alone qualifies a person to truly "get it." Parenting is one of those things.

Most of us grow up acknowledging that our parents loved us. Even when they embarrassed us, and even when we drove them crazy, we mentally accepted the fact that they loved us. Until a person becomes a parent, she cannot fully comprehend what it means to love her child unconditionally. When the first born child hits the one-month mark, many of us begin calling our parents to confess that we didn't really understand all they did to sacrifice and care for us.

AGES AND STAGES

I love the Red Sox; always have and always will. My daughter is actually a fifth generation Red Sox fan, so the love of baseball and the Red Sox goes deep in my family. It's great watching the power pitchers when they are young. They can throw in the mid to high 90s and dominate professional hitters. What's even more fun is watching an older pitcher, who has lost some of his velocity but has really learned to vary his pitch speeds, positions, and styles.

As we get older in youth ministry, we may lose some of our speed, but we will learn to use a variety of skills to achieve longevity and greater effectiveness in our ministry with students.

Many young youth ministers will not have the nerve to instruct parents of teenagers on how to better parent their teenagers, though some will charge forward anyway. Even if we didn't say it out loud, though, most of us who've been at this a while, back when we were younger and without children, were sure we were going to be the best parents ever. Part of God's sense of humor is to eventually have us recognize how much we don't know now about what we used to know for sure.

> Part of God's sense of humor is to eventually have us recognize how much we don't know now about what we used to know for sure.

The strengths of being young can often cover up some of the weaknesses of being young in youth ministry. I had tons of energy, desire, and even good biblical knowledge from a seminary. But at that stage I didn't have much wisdom. Wisdom comes from living life well—and from learning from our mistakes and the mistakes of others.

One of the best things we can do for our ministries is to gain more humility. This is true regardless of how long we've been in the game, but it is especially useful to cultivate early. My experience is that people who do not choose to be humble end up being humbled by others. So making the choice to pursue humility saves us a lot of pain and scars.

When I was 23, I taught a Sunday school class of 20 seventh grade boys. They were just like of a pack of squirrels. As one of them was picking his nose, I'd say, "You guys think you're cool, don't you?" And they'd all nod in the affirmative.

Then I'd drop 200 pounds of truth on their egos by saying, "No, you're not, and you know why? Nobody is cool in seventh grade. And if you doubt me, come see me in two to three years, and you'll realize how un-cool you were then."

The same could be said for most youth ministers within their first few years of ministry.

Part of being young is thinking we know more than we actually do, and that has been going on for a long time. Mark Twain once wrote, "When I was a boy of 14, my father was so ignorant I could hardly stand to have the old man around. But when I got to be 21, I was astonished at how much the old man had learned in seven years."

Within the glorious calling of youth ministry, we could say, "When I was a youth worker of 25, parents of teens were so ignorant I could hardly stand to have them around. But when I was a youth worker at 40, I was astonished at how much those parents of teens had learned in 15 years."

IN RETROSPECT

Fortunately, I was smart enough to avoid complaining to the senior pastor about our spiritually immature parents who were leading our students away from God by having them skip church to do homework. Unfortunately, I wasn't smart enough to properly hear from the parents and understand their perspective.

I wish I had done a better job listening to parents. No one knows their children better than their parents, and my ministry to young people would've been far more effective had I taken the time to listen to parents talk about their kids and their parenting, rather than just trying to pursue my agenda. These days, I always suggest to new youth ministers to meet regularly with parents one-on-one or in small groups just to ask them all kinds of questions that will help them better understand parents' experiences and concerns.

142 IT HAPPENS

More often, youth ministers are coming to understand their roles as ministers to youth and their families. Some churches even use titles like that, which I think is terrific. If I had my first few years of youth ministry to do over again, I would spend less energy trying to be the go-to guy for all of the kids' faith needs, and I'd spend more energy trying to partner with parents to help them live out the Deuteronomy 6 admonition to pass on their faith to their children.

Even youth ministers without teenage children of their own can find good resources about parenting teenagers. They can devour parenting books and suggest the good ones to parents. They can attend workshops on parenting teenagers, or host seminars at their churches. Part of being a good minister to youth and their families is to help connect parents to good resources. I don't have to be a parenting expert in order to provide books, training opportunities, web links, or other resources; I just have to be willing to look around at what's out there, cull through some of it, and pass on the best stuff.

QUESTIONS TO CONSIDER

Which parents of teenagers can I talk with to try and better understand what it means to be a parent of a teenager?

Where can I find another youth worker in my area who is a parent of a teenager that I can talk with?

In what ways might I come across as a know-it-all youth worker to the parents in my ministry?

How can I capitalize on whatever parenting and ministry experience level I'm in?

GONE
PARENTS WHO VOTE
WITH THEIR FEET

Doug Ranck, a youth ministry veteran of 30+ years, is the youth pastor at the Free Methodist Church in Santa Barbara, California. He's a regular writer for Interlinc's WriteGroup and staff consultant for Youth Ministry Architects. In addition he coordinates a local network of youth leaders while being actively involved with training and consulting youth leaders around Southern California.

When it comes to life outside of ministry, I'm an easy guy to surprise. My wife is regularly able to surprise me with gifts, guests, and sometimes, even trips. I most often do not pick up the clues. It is not my nature to dance merrily through life without planning or observing, but I'm especially gullible when it comes to unexpected fun.

That's in my personal life. In ministry, my profile is different. After three decades of ministry, though I still remain teachable, I have seen enough to be rarely surprised by events or responses of people. Ministry surprises seem to be more isolated.

There is one unhappy surprise for which I am seldom prepared.

THE SITUATION

Most recently this reminder came to me in a phone conversation with one of our parents. I had seen the family in Sunday worship with a fair amount of regularity but had not seen the teenager at our weekend or weekday meetings in awhile. For some time I assumed it was busyness—a realistic assumption these days. I checked with the student, and she confirmed my assumption.

Eventually, though, I came to the conclusion it was time to talk to the parents and let them know their daughter was missed—not to produce guilt but to express genuine pastoral concern. While talking with the mom on the phone, I let her know we would be excited to see her daughter after this hectic period concluded. What I expected to hear was, "Yes, thanks. We do appreciate your prayers, and our daughter really does love coming. It's great to know you are always there for the youth."

Instead I heard what is known as the "pregnant pause," immediately followed by these words: "Well…actually…our daughter is not coming for a different reason."

At this moment many things went through my head, including but not limited to:

1. I wish I could see the parent right now. I wish I could size up the non-verbal cues to prepare for the words ahead.

2. A quick mental listing of all the reasons, from best-case to worst-case scenarios, this mom may be going to offer me.
3. The overwhelming sensation of wanting to be on a Caribbean island, sitting in a lounge chair with water lapping at my feet and not a care in the world.

The mom then said, "Our daughter does not feel safe in the youth ministry. While I'm sure there are nice people who come to the youth group, she has been frequently ignored or sometimes belittled by a certain small group of girls. To her this feels no different than being at school, so for her welfare and happiness we have decided to have her just go to worship with us on Sunday mornings."

At this moment the "pregnant pause" is loud from my side of the phone.

How did this happen? What do I say? What should I say? How can I "fix" this? Am I really too young to retire? These and more questions were all running through my head during the eternal pause.

THE DILEMMA

I hear people say it is what we learn from our mistakes that count. I would love for this to never happen again, but I'm sure this is a test I can't say I have passed. It will happen again.

I will get blindsided again, and I'll need some strategy—and hope—for dealing with similar situations down the road. In preparing for that day, I should first note how I felt when this girl's mom dropped the "bomb" on me.

The first feeling was one of failure. How could I have let this happen? Where were the volunteer leaders when this was happening?

The second feeling was one of disappointment. Why did this parent or teenager not feel comfortable in telling us there was a problem?

The third feeling was a result of the second: anger. When the shock of the situation wore off, I found myself being angry at the parents for not letting me have the opportunity to respond to the situation before their daughter left.

MY RESPONSE

"Defensive" might be one word to summarize my response on the phone that day. I communicated my surprise to hear this situation had happened and talked about our stellar program where leaders care about kids. I stated how

I had not seen any indication of this incident and how frequent interactions with the girl had yielded no clues of this growing problem. I quickly added how we would have responded immediately if we had known.

After listening to me "blabber" for a while, the mom said, "I understand what you're saying, but the fact is that it did happen. There was no change, and now, for our daughter's emotional safety, we have removed her from the group. We have nothing against the church or you, but for now this is better."

I reiterated my previous points, not believing we could have been this wrong and sprinkled in a token apology.

The mother said no more. I thanked her for calling and we said goodbye.

TAKEAWAYS

After counsel with some trusted youth ministry teammates, my wife, my senior pastor and most importantly, God, I identified the following "takeaways":

1) I'm not perfect. Our ministry is not perfect.

2) I cannot control all relationships in the life of our ministry. When two people get together, there are two possible interactions, when three people get together there are six possible different points of communication. Imagine how many possible interactions there might be with even ten people?

3) I "hurdled" over the mom's comments and went straight to my agenda.

4) Talking about the excellence of your ministry means little when someone has experienced otherwise.

> Talking about the excellence of your ministry means little when someone has experienced otherwise.

5) Token apologies are hollow.

IN RETROSPECT

How I responded then and how I hope would respond now are marked by a deepening understanding of my humanness and utter dependence on God to humbly serve the Lord and shepherd those with whom I have been entrusted. The ministry of Jesus was one of recognizing his role and coming not to be served but to serve (Mark 10:45). Likewise, I aspire to remain humble in my position of authority so that I might more effectively grow in my own character and help others to do the same.

Here, then, is my ever-developing list of appropriate responses to this type of situation in the future:

1) **Let the ministry be the Lord's ministry.** To own this ministry for myself causes sleepless nights and defensive reactions toward those who find weakness. When I hold the ministry loosely and strive to be God's faithful servant rather than be the "king" of my little ministry fiefdom, I will be far less likely to be personally offended or hurt when the relationships of others are not going well. My compassion and care as a shepherd is appropriate; my defensiveness as an owner is not.

2) **Listen first.** My physical ears allowed noise to come in because I did not listen to what the mom was really trying to tell me. I have learned over the years when I am being confronted either in person or on the phone to grab a pad of paper. As the person is talking this allows me to write down a few key statements he or she is making. This offers two benefits: a) It also allows me to displace some of the anger, frustration, or hurt I may be feeling through the pen and onto the paper, and b) In the physical presence of the confronter it communicates I am listening and gives me notes for reflection later on when my emotional state has become more stable.

3) **A swift apology is a good beginning.** We rave about companies and stores offering immediate, no-questions-asked refunds on products we return. They often quickly apologize and ask how they can serve us better. This principle works well in ministry, too. While we may argue the need for apology, in certain situations the person bringing a complaint to us is expressing a perceived—and, in his or her eyes, legitimate—concern. An authentic apology addressing the concern will validate the complainant's feelings and open the door for more healthy interaction and reconciliation in the future.

> Token apologies are hollow. An authentic apology addressing the concern will validate the complainant's feelings and open the door for more healthy interaction and reconciliation in the future.

4) **Manage up.** Isolating ourselves in the midst of these circumstances leaves us lonely and vulnerable. When you first hear of any incident where safety or health in relationships has been compromised, communicate this to your immediate supervisor. Senior pastors would much rather hear about problems first from us so they may offer counsel and be prepared to respond effectively to any concerns ultimately reaching their desks. This also builds more trust with our most important teammate and helps us to see our "blind" spots.

5) **Commit to follow-up.** No conversation in this setting is complete without letting the person with concern know you will be following-up. In

using these words you affirm the hearing of his or her alarm, show your intention to understand it, and pledge to bring healing and wholeness to the situation and to the ministry in general.

6) **Seek reconciliation.** Be faithful in doing everything you can to bring resolution to situations where people have decided to "vote with their feet." Your efforts may or may not succeed in bringing about the result for which you would have hoped, but your intentions will be known and signal your *bona fide* care for the lives of the young people and their families.

QUESTIONS TO CONSIDER

In what ways do I think of my ministry as something I own rather than something I steward for God?

How well do I listen when people critique what is happening on my watch? How can I reduce defensiveness to that critique?

How can I learn from those who vote with their feet?

BOUNDARY ISSUES
WHEN VOLUNTEERS DATE
EACH OTHER

Troy Howley is the High School and Post-High School Group Life Pastor at Mars Hill Bible Church where he provides leadership and care for volunteers and small group relationships as well as crisis management for students. He lives with his wife, Kelley, and dog, Harper, in Grand Rapids, Michigan, where he just completed his M.Div.

Scott was a young volunteer—very eager to serve students and always available to hang out with them. He was a college graduate who grew up at the church and had been volunteering in the high school group for four years. The small group of students he led enjoyed spending time with him, and he enjoyed spending time with them. Katie was a college student at a local university; and although she had been plugged into the church community for the last three years, this was her first volunteering in the student ministry. She, too, was great with her students—she was a great listener and spoke profound truths.

Scott and Katie enjoyed regularly hanging out with the same group of friends; as the year progressed, they grew interested in each other and started to date. Scott's and Katie's dating relationship was very obvious in the youth group—they showed up to the group together, they left together, and they spent more time during the evening interacting. As they led their small groups, their students were also very familiar with the relationship—because these groups shared their lives together, the new romance was talked about regularly in both of their groups.

MY RESPONSE

While students and volunteers were fine, even excited about this relationship, I was concerned, even haunted, with the potential problems this relationship would create; and I came up with a list of questions: Are they committed to their students or to each other? Are they remaining pure? Is the relationship influencing their ability to lead? What will students' parents say about this? Will this impact the way their students view them?

Because of all of these concerns, I asked Scott and Katie to come in and talk with me.

As the youth leader, I felt it was my duty to clearly point out that there was nothing wrong with them dating, but rather, wanted to make sure that it wouldn't negatively impact the group. To do this, I imposed specific rules on the couple that I felt would protect our group.

After agreeing to these rules, Scott and Katie left the meeting. Little was spoken about this meeting for the remainder of the year, and because Scott and Katie had a healthy relationship (and followed the imposed rules), we never talked to them about their relationship again.

IN RETROSPECT

Guy likes girl. Girl likes guy. Guy and girl date. Happens all the time. Change the names in the story above, or modify their history a bit, and you probably are familiar with a similar situation.

Now the tricky part: what to do with these new relationships. In youth ministry volunteers dating one another can be the cause of many headaches and heartaches. Youth leaders must set boundaries and make sure that "everyone plays by the rules."

FEAR-BASED RULE SETTING

Unfortunately, looking back at this situation, I've come to realize that my perspective was fundamentally problematic. Defaulting to rule setting conveys a potentially painful posture toward leaders that communicates, "I don't trust you, and I'm scared that you are going to mess up." It conveys a posture of fear.

> Defaulting to rule setting conveys a potentially painful posture toward leaders that communicates, "I don't trust you, and I'm scared that you are going to mess up." It conveys a posture of fear.

Certainly, precautions should be taken, but these should be outlined early and for all volunteers—not just ones entering into a romantic relationship. Whether volunteers are married, in a relationship, or single, they should be expected to respect each other and those around them, promoting safety for volunteers and students alike. Setting these guidelines ahead of time allows the volunteers to understand what is and isn't appropriate within the youth group before they are put in a confusing situation. Targeting specific individuals, however, based solely on relationship status, does not breed trust or love, but rather mistrust and fear.

BOUNDARY ISSUES **155**

Fortunately, Scott and Katie didn't get frustrated with me; and they followed my request as they continued to serve. Still I wonder what would happen if they did feel hurt? Or if they were struggling and needed support? What then? In my fear-based rule setting, I failed to respect them as volunteers.

SUPPORT OVER RULES

In many cases, youth leaders may be too quick to place rules and expectations upon newly-dating volunteers—it is not appropriate to be a "couple" while in the youth room; make sure you have healthy boundaries, etc. (and I must note that these are not necessarily bad things)—but perhaps any rule by itself fails to support couples before, during, or after the dating process.

Rules can never help a couple when they have an argument right before youth group. Nor do they help when the couple has a messy breakup and still both serve in the same group. They can never help a couple figure out what an appropriate relationship looks like within the youth group.

This is why the youth minister should frame his or her role in these relationships as a supporter rather than a rule-enforcer. Instead of focusing on what they *can't* do, perhaps we should mentor them or set them up with a mentoring older leader to better learn what they *can* do. It is safe to assume that relationships, in general, are good. The creation narrative establishes this. Therefore, as opportunity arises, teach and guide volunteers into understanding what healthy relationships look like.

Creating an environment in which the youth leader is available and willing to talk to volunteers about their lives in and outside of the youth room allows for support to happen. If the only time volunteers speak to their leader is when they "break the rules," they are being greatly mistreated.

HEALTHY EXPECTATIONS, PROPER TIMING

Perhaps it is a good thing when two volunteers begin dating—maybe one of the best ways to meet someone is through a mutual desire to serve a certain group of people like a youth group. This does not mean that every relationship that pops up is a great fit, nor does it mean that youth leaders should become matchmakers. In shepherding volunteers, a youth leader ought to celebrate the former and discourage the latter. This can only be done, however, if clear expectations are offered.

Situations like Scott and Katie have helped me realize that youth leaders should handle each volunteer relationship differently. First, expectations must be established with volunteers at the beginning of the year with all relationships. This can be done through trainings at the beginning of the year on a variety of different topics (including aspects of relationships—be them between friends, volunteers and students, or in romantic endeavors). It is also hugely beneficial to give a field manual to each volunteer that includes expectations of them throughout the year. Again, giving expectations at the beginning of the year can save leaders, volunteers, and students from confusion down the line.

Second, when two leaders begin to date, we should not default to rule setting. Instead, we should establish a support system to help young couples navigate serving in our ministries and growing closer together as a couple. In our ministry, we have volunteers (called Family Leaders) who care for the volunteers who care for students. These Family Leaders know what is going on in the lives of our other volunteers, pray for them, and help them navigate life—both as a volunteer and as a person. The specific support structure will vary from church to church, but we should all ensure that someone in our ministries seeks to know the couple and is regularly talking with the couple about their ministry progress and dating relationship.

Adult volunteer relationships happen. While we have necessary parameters to protect other volunteers and watching students, we also have something to celebrate if two people find each other while serving God. The art of pastoring is to resist giving ridged, cold rules based on fear, and to offer relational support that encourages healthy interaction before, during, and after a dating relationship.

QUESTIONS TO CONSIDER

What rules do I have in place regarding romantic relationships among volunteers? Which ones are based in fear and should be re-thought? Which are based in wisdom or experience and should be reinforced?

What rules about other things have I developed that are fear-based? Experientially-based? Are there ones that need to be re-considered, nuanced, or even expunged?

What kinds of support structures do I have in place to encourage, strengthen, and support the adult volunteers who pour into the lives of my kids? What additional support structures do we need to add?

TOO CLOSE
FOR COMFORT
OPPOSITE-GENDER RELATIONSHIPS

Danette Matty has been volunteering with teenagers and young adults since big hair was in. In 2010 she crash-landed into full-time ministry in Nebraska with her husband and two teenagers, where she is the Director of Christ's Place Leadership College, a mentoring program for emerging leaders. She's a published author, freelance writer, and part of Group's National Training Team.

I am amazed by how the enemy of our souls can take a legitimate, but manageable, issue and magnify it in our thinking so that we are convinced it's overwhelming.

Several years ago, my husband and I hit a rough patch in our friendship. Money was tight. We were tense. We both turned to our default modes: he, in controlling things; me, turning inward. We didn't yell. We didn't throw things. In our interactions, it was just avoid, resent, repeat.

Because of what I'm about to share, my husband and I came clean about our poor coping mechanisms. We ended up on the other side of the gravel with sturdier tire treads and a deeper bond. We are now quicker to turn full face toward each other when we're tempted to cope with frustration in unhealthy ways.

But our boundaries were tested back then. And as humbling as it is to tell you this story, if you'll learn from my mistakes, then I have nothing to lose.

WHAT HAPPENED

At the time, a close friend and fellow youth worker I'll call Rob began to notice my frustration and then listen and empathize. I justified pouring my heart out to him based on the desire to get a male perspective. Though we loved our spouses and were committed to our marriages, relational tension was on the rise in both our homes. Slowly, he and I began to share too many details about our marriages and internal struggles...things that should have been reserved for accountability with a trusted same-gender friend.

Rob and I clicked, understood each other, and cheered each other on in youth work. We eased the strain of ministry by laughing, comparing life experience notes, and encouraging each other. But we acted out the adage: "A hungry need is a dangerous need." I was needy, and Rob—perhaps mutually needy, though likely unintentionally—fed my sentimental appetite.

I knew we'd crossed a line one night—ironically, in the wake of a powerful youth service. I was dealing with my personal struggles, including said marital frustration.

As youth group dismissed and kids started to leave, I tucked myself backstage, crying and praying. Later, spotting me in the near empty parking lot, Rob motioned for me to sit in his vehicle before I went home. He had seen me crying and asked why. I pointed to another female youth worker sitting in my car, waiting for a ride home. (Smart move, Danette.) I told Rob, "I know I can tell you anything, but I've been crying. Let's talk another time when I'm not so emotional." (So far, so good.)

But Rob didn't let it go. I think his motives were pure; I was, after all, a fellow youth leader. He looked me in the eye and said in a soft, sincere voice, "She can wait. Talk to me." (Not so smart move, Rob.) We ended up talking longer as I shared my marital dissatisfaction and love hunger. I think Rob felt like he was being a good friend, having earned the distinct place of hearing these very private details and sympathizing.

Let's pause here and state a simple truth: this conversation might not have been the hook in my heart toward Rob had it taken place, as I'd initially suggested, in a day or two, after my emotions had subsided. A little wisdom and stick-to-my-common-sense-guns would have thwarted the attachment to Rob I felt after that talk.

Looking back, I recall a pang of guilt after bad-mouthing my husband. I sensed the uncut questioning of the Holy Spirit: "Is he really that bad, or does it just feel good to have someone coddle you right now?"

> What began as genuine, Christ-honoring camaraderie morphed into a tender, passionate, melodramatic bond of sacred secrets.

What began as genuine, Christ-honoring camaraderie morphed into a tender, passionate, melodramatic bond of sacred secrets. It was only a matter of time before I became physically attracted to him. When that happens, the deceptive feeling of "safety" is utterly dangerous.

Through a combination of God's grace and what few reserves of healthy boundaries we managed not to violate, no physical affair took place—but emotional boundaries were crossed, for sure. Dr. Kara Powell, author and executive director of Fuller Youth Institute, talks about "emotional affairs" in youth ministry (two decades ago, Jeanne Mayo called it emotional adultery): "You're sharing the experience of lives being changed, you're excited about what God's doing, and you're passionate about your work. It's easy to let that passion spill over into unhealthy relationships with opposite sex volunteers or paid coworkers." Powell says it may not be physical, "but you're flirting with an equally explosive form of intimacy."

Danger #1: A False Sense of Boundaries

Rob and I never touched each other inappropriately, and I wasn't in love with him. But therein lies the danger. Is sustained eye contact adultery if there's no kiss? How does sharing intimate details about one's married life influence attraction? Surely there's no connection. Or is there?

> Is sustained eye contact adultery if there's no kiss?

Proverbs 10:19 says, "Too much talk leads to sin. Be sensible and keep your mouth shut."

My marital angst had nothing to do with Rob. I shouldn't have cracked that emotional door with him. Once I began talking, it was easy to exaggerate whatever I felt was missing from my friendship with my husband. And once those words came out, I should have gone back to Rob and said, "Thanks for being a great listener. I'm afraid I felt so comfortable that I went on and on about my husband. In hindsight, I may have exaggerated the drama a little. That wasn't fair to him or you, and it was completely inappropriate. I'm sorry. I don't want the devil to get a foothold in our mission to shepherd teenagers. Let's keep our conversations focused on that." And then I should have determined to sort this heavy stuff out with an accountability partner and my husband.

Danger #2: A False Sense of Sanctity

Late night conversations in an empty parking lot all by ourselves. What were we thinking? The same thing one might think of any close ministry friend who confides too much; we assume it's a one-time conversation and that because he loves Jesus, he's going to take steps to remedy his behavior or thought patterns.

Here's the kicker: during this time frame, spiritual disciplines were evident in my life. I regularly read the Bible and engaged in time alone with Jesus. I was immersed in Danger #2. I was certain in my heart that nothing questionable would happen between Rob and me. He had made enough statements to affirm the same of his own desire to be pure. Regardless of what we felt we lacked in our marriages, we were smart enough to know an affair wasn't the answer. So boundary pushing didn't feel as dangerous as it was.

I think there's more than one reason Jesus admonished his followers saying, "You have heard that it was said, 'You shall not commit adultery.' But I tell you that anyone who looks at a woman lustfully has already committed

162 IT HAPPENS

> Sin is committed one seemingly innocuous step at a time—from the mind to the heart to the mouth to the hands.

adultery with her in his heart" (Matthew 5.27-30 NIV). Sin is committed one seemingly innocuous decision at a time—from the mind to the heart to the mouth to the hands.

IN RETROSPECT

By way of circumstances and to my relief, some distance came between Rob and me. I repented to God—and to my husband—for straying from him emotionally and gossiping about him to Rob. He asked me to forgive him for not being clued into my needs. A couple of pastor's wives came alongside me with a commitment to walk with me in the aftermath of my emotional stupidity. Since then, I have done my best to live by a set of boundaries for which I'm accountable to my husband and select sister-friends who love me enough to let me expose my sins in their safe and prayerful care.

Honesty

We can't avoid getting close with people we work with. But we can be butt-ugly honest about the type of person you could be attracted to.

Tell yourself the truth about this. After all, there will always be someone who is, does, or has something your spouse isn't, doesn't, or doesn't have—he or she will laugh at your jokes, be better looking, more spiritual, less demanding, or fill-in-the-blank-with-whatever.

A pastor I know interviewed people for the open secretarial position at his church. He chose not to hire one woman in particular because she carried herself with just enough sensuality that he didn't want to invite that into the office and into his life. When you sense there is a certain spiritual, emotional, or sensual attraction, be like Joseph and get the hell out. Literally, when you "flee from youthful lusts" (2 Timothy 2:22), you get hell's grip out of your life!

Spiritualization

Don't spiritualize your motives by having selective boundaries, where you maintain a double standard with someone you consider safe. Sure, some people who are "like a brother or sister" are easier to talk to than others. But, as Powell points out, if you're just plain busy, hungry for attention, or desperate for affirmation, you may open up to that person one unguarded time too many. "Across denominations, men and women are having emotional affairs,"

Powell states. "They're staying out of bed and not abandoning their families, but their coworkers have become surrogate spouses."

Accountability

Be accountable. "But, accountability isn't in the Bible." Really? That's your rationale for keeping hidden sin in safe harbor? Put on your big kid pants and call someone. You cannot underestimate the value of a trusted friend who knows your susceptibility and will talk and pray you through temptation.

Whenever I speak at ministry events, particularly out of town, I email a group of people to request prayer. Then I send a separate email to two trusted women to whom I have committed honesty in this area of my life. I briefly share how I'm spending my free time, what I'm watching on TV, how I'm interacting with male colleagues, and most importantly, what's going on in my head. That's being proactive with James' instruction to "confess your sins to each other and pray for each other so that you may be healed" (James 5:16 NIV).

Sin flourishes in darkness. When we bring our temptations and propensities into the light, God's grace diminishes their power and brings healing to our sin-sickness.

H.A.L.T.

Evangelist Pat Schatzline uses the acronym H.A.L.T. to describe a state in which we are prone to make bad decisions. We should be especially vigilant when we are **H**ungry, **A**ngry, **L**onely, or **T**ired. When our defenses are down for any reason, we have to be smarter than our flesh. We should slow down (or completely halt) in order to listen to the whispered prompting of God's Spirit.

Flee Gossip

Criticizing your spouse might invite sympathy, but unless you are complaining to someone who knows and loves you *and your spouse*, you are gossiping and violating your spouse's trust. Pastor Rick Lorimer says, "The line is subtle and slow. If it were a brick hitting you over the head, it wouldn't be so easy to cross that line." Don't cross that line in conversation with someone of the opposite sex or one who isn't a trusted advisor or friend.

Proverb 4:23 (NLT) says, "Guard your heart above all else, for it determines the course of your life." When we move from Christ-honoring talk to throwing out feelers or sending signals for hidden reasons, our conversation immediately goes from appropriate to inappropriate. Word pictures are easily planted, and flames could be fanned that weren't there before.

The enemy of your soul and your marriage would love nothing more that to lead you to a confidant who has the same issues in his or her marriage. Mutually hazardous neediness, anyone?

Keep intimacy in your bedroom and out of the office. The more open the topic of sex becomes in casual conversation, the less value it has to us.

Appearance of Impropriety

Watch your step. Follow the same advice you would give your students about physical boundaries—not only for your sake, but for the sake of people who could easily misread the situation.

A friend told me that while finishing her degree, she would, with her husband's knowledge and approval, share a ride to the college with their mutual friend who was driving the same way. It never dawned on my friend that this could be seen as anything other than frugality until during a block party her neighbor wondered out loud, "Who is that guy you're having an affair with?"

Years ago, I lived in a small town. I used to jog up to our little church to pray during the day, when there wasn't much activity going on. Our bivocational pastor occasionally stopped in to work for a few hours. As much as he appreciated a parishioners' commitment to prayer, he eventually asked me to call before showing up so we wouldn't be at the church at the same time with no one around. He was thinking beyond our pure motives about how neighbors could use their imagination to conjure up accusations.

Two good rules of thumb:

1. Don't be alone with someone of the opposite sex in a car, home, or office.
2. If you're a tactile person, it may be hard to forego; but with the opposite gender, limit your warm-fuzzy touches to handshakes and shoulders, or not at all.

MOVING FORWARD

Does this mean I have no opposite gender friends? Of course not. But my closest male friends are godly men who either a) are also friends with my husband, or b) behave with unspoken but obvious boundaries that make them safe, or both.

We don't have to swing the pendulum to the legalistic extreme, but we do need to be hyper vigilant about our opposite-gender relationships—not only for the sake of our marriages but also for the sake of our witness to others. As my small town pastor explained to me, "I don't really care what people think about me. But I do care what they think about the Lord."

QUESTIONS TO CONSIDER

In what ways do I look for emotional fulfillment in people I shouldn't?

In what ways do I play the "How far is too far?" game, hoping to push the boundaries out as far as possible? What is a more spiritually mature perspective?

Are there unguarded relationships in my life right now? If so, what do I need to do about it? If not, how can I prevent them arising?

Do I find reasons to visit a colleague's office just to hang out? Do I continue talking about random things after I've received an answer to my question or finished a conversation with him or her?

Do I check my appearance to make sure I look nice in front of someone to whom I'm attracted?

Do I see inappropriate relationships within my sphere of influence? Without overstepping my own boundaries, how am I being called to speak difficult words of truth to others?

CROSSING THE LINE
WHEN VOLUNTEERS DATE KIDS

Mark Montgomery is an ordained youth minister in the Church of England, and the Youth officer for the Diocese of Chester. A contributing editor to *Young People and Worship: a Practical Guide*, he spends his time training, teaching, and mentoring youth ministers, consulting with churches, speaking at youth events, studying trends in youth ministry, and writing resources.

I pick up the phone, glad to hear that it's John, a pastor friend of mine from one of the local churches I support. After the usual catch up about family and life, he gets to the point of his call, which is a lot more serious than our normal conversations. I can hear in his voice he is a little tentative when bringing up the situation.

Judy, the church's gap-year (or intern) youth leader has started to date one of the kids in the group. Apparently, they are very much in love; and, apparently, the relationship has been going on for a while.

It only came to light when one of the other youth leaders on the team raised some questions about how much time Judy and this boy were spending together. Other leaders had also noticed that Judy always picked this boy to do things in the sessions over and above other members of the group.

My friend John was a little unsure what to do. Judy is 18, and the kid is 17. Other church kids of similar ages are dating, and no one has a problem. He was surprised he hadn't noticed this going on before, but as a busy pastor he had trusted Judy with the youth ministry and thought she knew the boundaries of the role. I could hear the disappointment in his voice.

As he asks the next question, I think he already knows the answer. But he asks it anyway: Should he treat this relationship differently because Judy is a youth leader, or should he just let it go like other relationships in the youth group?

DILEMMAS

Over the past few years I have had several similar conversations with pastors in my area—too often for my comfort. And this issue doesn't just crop up with gap-year students. Sometimes a volunteer youth leader begins dating a student; other times a young full-time youth minister develops a relationship. Occasionally, a senior, who is already dating a junior, graduates and becomes a leader—so the relationship developed prior to the leadership position.

This isn't a new situation in youth ministry; volunteers and youth ministers

169

have been falling for kids for decades. Sometimes they end in life-long relationships; but in many cases careers are ruined, marriages get wrecked, or even worse. So we have to be careful how we treat these situations.

> Volunteers and youth ministers have been falling for kids for decades. Sometimes they end in life-long relationships; but in many cases careers are ruined, marriages get wrecked, or even worse.

THE BIGGER ISSUE

One of the causes stems from the way we train youth leaders. We are usually good at training people about typical leadership tasks, but we don't talk much about the *costs* of leadership. When we accept the call to lead God's people, certain parts of our lives are not our own anymore. Certain life decisions have to be taken wearing a leadership hat, not just a personal one. This is one of the harsh realities of being in Christian ministry—and especially youth ministry.

Rarely do I meet young leaders who are aware of this. They are typically caught up in the passion of doing the work today rather than the difficult sacrifices necessary to sustain it for the long haul.

Was it Judy's fault that she crossed the boundary of leadership and child protection and became romantically involved with a kid in the group? Or was it the church's fault for not telling her this situation should never have happened in the first place, however normal it may seem amongst her friends?

Abraham knew the harsh realities of being a leader. In Genesis 22 we read an account of God testing Abraham by asking him to take his son Isaac to a place to be sacrificed. Abraham had been waiting for a son for many years, and after God had finally given him one, it seems that God was going to take Isaac away from him. Abraham feared the Lord, though, and was willing to follow God whatever the cost. Not until the last minute did God stop Abraham from sacrificing Isaac, his 'son, his only son that he loves' (22:2).

Leadership comes at a cost. Our ministries are going to test us at times.

> Leadership comes at a cost.

Certain young people in our groups may become attractive to us, seeming to offer us things our current relationships don't. When this occurs, we need to stand firm in our faith and make sure we act appropriately. We might be flattered by the attention we receive, but we should flee from such thoughts and actions quickly and without hesitation. We should be aware that we have to make decisions as youth ministers that affect our lives outside of our ministries.

In 1 Tim: 3 we read Paul's qualifications of Bishops and Deacons. Paul sets high standards on what it means to serve in these roles. The qualifications of a deacon offer guidance regarding appropriate behavior for those in leadership. The Greek word *diakonos*, from which we get the term "deacon" means "servant," "minister," or "messenger."

The qualifications listed by Paul cost us, both inside and outside our ministries. On more than one occasion, we might like to go out and get drunk with friends and forget about the cares of the world for a while. But that one action may carry ramifications that would affect young people's (and their parents') perceptions of us for a long, long time. Sometimes we may have to exclude ourselves from things or go home early and look like the killjoy.

If we are to be held blameless when tested (by new potential employers and church members) we need to demonstrate ministries that are free of any questionable actions.

One of the big doubts that hang over any youth minister for a long time is the issue of inappropriate relationships with young people. These inappropriate relationships might start off innocently—but even minor transgressions can cost a career. If relationships between leaders (regardless of their ages) and youth are regarded as acceptable by the leadership team, then you will encourage a place where inappropriate relationships are the norm in your youth ministry.

HOW I RESPONDED

As I listened to John, I knew that some of the questions I was about to ask him were going to strain our friendship. They are the same questions that I would ask any youth minister who came with the situation of a volunteer who was starting to date a kid:

- Has anyone ever told the leader that this is wrong or shouldn't happen?
- Has the leader ever been through Safe Sanctuaries or other child protection training?
- What other training was given to the leader before starting the role?
- Has the leader's role been specifically spelled out in some type of agreement?
- Have the leader been taught about the personal cost and sacrifice that leadership entails?

These can be hard questions, especially as they can reach into and question deeply the Pastor's role in setting up the youth leader's job. John explained that he assumed Judy knew what the boundaries were and that she had undertaken youth ministry training prior to being approved as a leader. The assumptions made by John are commonplace, unfortunately.

Not many people spell out the expectations of what is appropriate and what is not, and what it means to take on a leadership role in the church. Over the past decade in the United Kingdom, we have seen a move to start recruiting volunteers in a similar way to full-time youth ministry workers and clearly spelling out what is expected of them.

If John had done this with Judy, she would have known what was appropriate—and that the relationship she had started with the kid in the group was not and never would be. I explained to John that if this were in a school, Judy were a young teacher, and she were having a relationship with a pupil, we wouldn't be having a conversation like this. It's not just full-timers or gappers, but volunteers, as well; we need to clearly state what the boundaries are. If the youth leaders are not happy with these terms, they need to step down from their roles.

Judy was left to make a hard decision: should she end the relationship with the kid in the group or step down from her position? If she steps down and wants to continue her youth ministry career she would have to answer questions about why she stepped down from her position for many years to come. Her explanation would likely create doubt around her ministry, and she would be open to serious questions.

During our residential and events programs, we encourage young leaders (16-18 year olds) to work on the planning teams and at the events—but we spell out a couple of things to them and the other leaders. Once they take on the role of a leader, we expect them to refrain from getting romantically involved with any of the young people at the event. Likewise, to the older leaders—although these young people are acting as part of our leadership team, they are still young people in our care, so romantic relationships between them are out of bounds, as well. Sometimes the roles can get mixed up, especially for people in the middle, not quite young people and not quite leaders. So we are very specific in making sure everyone knows there roles and responsibilities.

It might sound harsh, especially in a church setting, but when we clearly know our expectations and boundaries, we can better work as a team and glorify God. Clear communication also allows us to question each other's practice, especially if we think things are going in a dodgy direction. I want to make

> When we clearly know our expectations and boundaries, we can better work as a team and glorify God.

sure the young leaders I am developing know from the outset what it means to be in church leadership—and what joys, responsibilities, and costs come along with that.

Some realize leadership is not for them at that moment, or not for them at all. Others recognize God's long-term call on their lives. For those, God has entrusted our leadership team with the responsibility to help them be successful. If we don't clearly communicate our expectations and boundaries, we set them up to stumble through their leadership—and sometimes completely fall.

WHAT I WOULD DO DIFFERENTLY

A few months later, John called me again to update me on the situation. The church had reviewed all their volunteer agreements in their youth and children's ministry. They had made sure that everyone was well aware of their roles and responsibilities and what was appropriate behavior. They had made sure all the leaders participated in child protection training and that any young leaders were being trained in an appropriate way so that this type of situation wouldn't happen again.

Judy decided that her long-term calling was to youth ministry, so she ended the relationship and sought out appropriate training. The cost to her leadership was that she had to separate herself from the kid she was dating, stand apart from her peers in the church, and recognize that God's calling on her life was more important than her relationship with another person. She accepted the cost of Christian leadership.

QUESTIONS TO CONSIDER

Have I considered the costs of Christian leadership? What boundaries do I tend to push that need to be solidified?

In what creative ways can I help train others regarding appropriate boundaries beyond a list of dos and don'ts?

What barriers stand between clear communication of expectations and boundaries to all leaders—both paid and volunteer, regardless of age—and how can I overcome them those barriers?

CROSSING OVER
COMING OUT OF THE CLOSET

Dave Wright is the Coordinator for Youth Ministry in the Diocese of South Carolina. He has been in full time youth ministry for 25 years, ten in a large church near Chicago, five in a medium sized church in Cheshire England, and ten years in South Carolina. Dave has written numerous articles for *YouthWork Magazine* (UK) as well as *Youthworker Journal* and led training in the UK, Canada, and USA.

Allan approached me after church one Sunday and said, "I need to have a word with you." The look on his face suggested that we ought to move away from the crowd of people around us.

A few moments later, he looked left and right and then straight into my eyes, took a deep breath, and said, "I want you to hear this from me directly rather than through the grapevine." He paused and asked, "How do I put this?"

After another pause, he continued, "Let me put this in terms that you as an American can relate to. I am batting for the other team." He seemed anxious to be relieved of this conversation and hoped I would understand without further explanation.

I decided to play dumb and replied with, "Are you playing baseball or cricket?"

Allan then suggested a saloon door metaphor, saying, "I am swinging the other way."

I felt it was important for him to state clearly what he needed to say, so I just asked him at that point to tell me straight out. Finally, Allan said, "I'm gay," at which point I confessed that I knew what he meant by the first metaphor but told him I wanted to hear him say it straight up. Then we both laughed at my unintentional pun.

THE DILEMMAS

I never expected to hear those words from someone who had been a volunteer on my leadership team for several years. At the same time, I was not shocked or surprised. The previous day, I had received a call from my pastor who was very concerned about this young man coming out, so I knew what Allan was going to say before he opened his mouth. Word was spreading at the church, and the pastor was fearful that this would have a negative impact on our ministry.

We were a conservative, evangelical church in a very un-churched area. Our youth ministry was the only active youth ministry within at least ten miles. We were reaching teens from the community whose parents were not believers. What would those parents think? How might they respond to the thought that one of our leaders had been secretly gay? Would they be concerned that we had put their boys in harm's way?

My concerns were slightly different. I was not thinking about the local people and the reputation of the ministry as much as how we as a community of believers were going to respond to the news. Allan had been a leader for several years, having started before I arrived on the scene. He was incredibly helpful through the leadership transition and helped me get acclimated in British youth culture. When I heard slang terms with which I was unfamiliar, Allan was my "go to" guy. He was a much-loved member of the team.

We playfully teased him when he "ran like a girl" or overreacted to the presence of a spider. He laughed at me when I used American expressions that carry a different meaning in England. It was not hard to notice that Allan was a bit flamboyant and effeminate. However, I have never been one to assume that such mannerisms equate to homosexual orientation. Allan was at my house all the time for Bible studies, leadership meetings, and Saturday night Ultimate Frisbee games. My wife and young kids loved him and looked forward to seeing him.

Allan joined the youth group years before, when he became friends with the pastor's son at school. A few years later, he went away to university for a semester before transferring to be closer to home. He joined the leadership team as a college student and was not all that many years older than the teens. His major was theology, and his career intent for a while was ministry; though that eventually changed without much explanation from him. Allan had a strong relational ministry with several of the guys in our group. He loved to talk theology and was a student of Scripture. In so many ways, he was an ideal leader in our ministry.

> Allan had a strong relational ministry with several of the guys in our group. He loved to talk theology and was a student of Scripture. In so many ways, he was an ideal leader in our ministry.

After about five years on our team, Allan called me one day to resign as a leader. He did not seem to have much reason for doing so, or at least I thought the reason given was weak. I asked him to stay on through until the end of the school year. My request of leaders has always been to complete a school year. He seemed to squirm at the thought of that. I asked him if there were any reason he could not finish the year; sheepishly he said "no" and agreed to stay on. There were only two months left in the semester during which he was around a bit less. A few weeks later, he came out.

Given my pastor's concern for the impact on parents and the reputation of the church, I gladly let him handle damage control via concerns that

CROSSING OVER **179**

people raised. It was his role as pastor of the church to deal with information that could be spread as rumors or gossip. He was more than willing to address this where and when it was needed. Because Allan came out during a summer break and after he resigned as a leader, the impact was very minimal. Things likely would have been different had he come out earlier. If that had been the case, there was no question that he would have been asked to step down.

Allan knew that. Our church's position on homosexuality was very clear. What was less clear was how we would love Allan and care for him pastorally. The pastor, having known him for nearly ten years, spent some time talking and praying with him. From Allan's comments later, I am not sure how well that was received. I am confident that it was handled in a firm but loving pastoral manner. I had further conversations with Allan, and he was quick to voluntarily assure me that his orientation did not play into his relationships with the youth group. He knew my position on the matter of his sexuality, but I also wanted to be crystal clear that it did not change my view of him nor diminish my love for him as a brother in Christ.

It sounds cliché to ask, "What would Jesus do?" But that was the approach we took with the young people when they raised questions about Allan's announcement. We explained to them that we viewed the Bible as being very

> It sounds cliché to ask, "What would Jesus do?" But that was the approach we took.

clear that homosexuality is not God's intention for humanity and that such behavior is considered a sin. At the same time, we hold to a theology that all of us are sinners by nature and that Jesus died for sinners. So, the WWJD response is no different for Allan than it is to anyone else. We are to love him as Jesus loves him.

While providing a teachable moment, the issue was at the same time not a big deal. Most of the students in our group knew people who had come out. Their culture was already more or less indifferent to the matter. This was perhaps one of the most eye-opening moments in my time at that church. In many other contexts, the whole episode would have created massive chaos at that point in time. Today, our American culture is somewhat indifferent to someone coming out; so in a way, we have caught up to where Britain was ten years ago.

IN RETROSPECT

Looking back, I see that things could have been different had I spent more time exploring his decision to resign before the end of the school year. I suspect had he resigned earlier, we would have had a greater mess to deal with because his departure would have been oddly timed and needed explaining. It might have forced him to come out before he was ready to do so. I also think there were a number of issues that we did not address fully.

In the context of relational ministry, we need to be aware of the issues of betrayal, hurt, anger, trust, and disappointment. We did not know how long Allan had been keeping his news inside of himself and betraying himself. When he did come out, we never discussed the feelings of betrayal some of us experienced as members of the leadership team. While we did not openly discuss grace, it was certainly tested by the situation. My observation was that our church for the most part, being a very close community, was very graceful in responding to the news. Yet, that did not prevent Allan from leaving the area and changing churches due his knowledge about our theological position on homosexuality.

Beyond going into damage control mode, we had an opportunity as a team, along with the leadership of the church, to really wrestle with the theological and practical implications of this event. Sadly the fact that it happened at summer break when people are constantly away, meant some of these things never got addressed. In the end, though, I am thankful for this leadership experience. I know that it molded my character in a way that has enabled me to respond to other challenges with grace and truth.

QUESTIONS TO CONSIDER

Do I agree with my church's views on the fundamental aspects of my faith? How do I reconcile any differences?

Am I clear regarding my perspective on hot-button issues like homosexuality, especially regarding those in ministry leadership?

In what ways am I consistent or inconsistent regarding other attributes of leaders in my ministry?

How well am I balancing grace with high standards?

JUST ONE MORE THING

ADDING NEW JOB RESPONSIBILITIES

Heather Shaw is a former youth leader who loves helping youth and families grow in faith. She attended Eastern University in St. Davids, Pennsylvania, and graduated with a degree in youth ministry. She is now a stay at home mom and is using her passions for bringing faith to life with her own "small group" of two young boys.

"Would you mind taking on the Elementary youth programs? Just for the summer?"

I had been hired part time to cover only middle and high school youth, and the families with younger children naturally felt neglected. The volunteers and parents weren't happy, and the pastors were looking for quick compromise. A little voice in my head told me it wasn't a good idea: I couldn't possibly do birth through 12th grade programming well in my 20-hour work week. Besides, I knew that once I took it on, it wouldn't be "just for the summer."

> A little voice in my head told me it wasn't a good idea.

Nonetheless, I cautiously said yes, and the pastor and I both agreed that my time would be stretched and I would have to carefully balance my tasks.

When I was hired a month earlier, the church was finishing up a building renovation program. Seemingly poised for growth, they had redefined the youth leader's role. Burnout was a key concern, so they split the youth leader's position into two part-time positions, a Director and an Administrator. The Administrator was in charge of…well, administration, while I was to focus on programming, developing volunteers, and creating a family ministry.

During my interview, I asked how much time each week they envisioned me spending with youth going to sports activities, out for coffee, etc. The pastors told me that I wouldn't have much time for relationship building with youth—they wanted a broad base of adult leaders who cared for the youth and not a "youth leader centered" program. I was pleased with their strong emphasis on staying balanced, focusing on priorities, and not taking on too much.

COMPLICATIONS

Shortly after the building project was finished, I realized that they had done so with an "if we build it, they will come" mentality—no plans were in place for outreach. Additionally, the economy took a downturn, and money became tight. Finally, the church voted over a controversial topic, and as a result a number of families left the church, further hurting their finances.

The pastors and church council entered a panic mode where they focused

184   IT HAPPENS

on the budget and attendance. We chased after gimmicks to increase atten-
dance, and being relevant became the main focus rather than the Gospel of
Jesus. Sermons shifted to a "moral gospel" rather than about the power of
Christ in our lives.

The youth ministry also suffered from this panic mode. I was asked to
take on more responsibilities to increase attendance and appease complaining
church members who had their own expectations of what I should be doing.
In addition to elementary, middle, and high school youth programming, volunteer development, and launching a family ministry, I was asked to work in
the nursery. Then, I was asked to participate in leading services.

Contrary to my interview, I was told to socialize with youth outside of
church activities. I was asked to teach and organize Sunday school classes for
parents. I was to lead a youth room renovation. I planned intergenerational
activities. Oh, and this was still to be done in 20 hours per week. They had
worked so hard to redefine the position before hiring me, and in the end they
did not even follow the job description.

Towards the end, in a job review, I discovered the church council didn't
even fully know what my job description was or how broad my responsibilities had become. They were upset that I had (seemingly) been neglecting the
middle school and high school youth, when I was under the assumption that
the pastor and I had agreed on where my energies would be focused. As it
turned out, even though the pastor and I had discussed this a few weeks earlier, she had "forgotten."

MY RESPONSE

When most youth ministers get a job, they are given a job description, which
is good. In a short amount of time, many realize that, regardless of what the
paper says, everyone has his or her own expectation of what those responsibilities should be. Even more difficult is the fact that most expectations
are unspoken. Because I wanted to be a team
player, saying no to added responsibilities was
difficult.

> Because I wanted to be a team player, saying no to added responsibilities was difficult.

Additionally, because the church was struggling, I naturally wanted to do what I could to
help turn it around. I tried to balance new responsibilities given to me while
staying focused on my priorities.

Knowing my tendencies to take on too much, I developed a plan of action: while maintaining programming with all ages, I'd focus extra energy on one age group at a time to strengthen the program. My pastor agreed this was a wise use of my time. In our weekly meetings, I would share what my leadership team and I had decided and ask if there was any feedback. I always got very positive feedback, so I thought all was well.

I also thought that what we were discussing was being shared with the church council to keep them in the loop. I was wrong.

Additionally, I tried to say no to extra responsibilities and stick to my priorities, as I had been encouraged to do in the beginning—but now the pastor was requiring the additional responsibilities.

IN RETROSPECT

I eventually left because we moved for my husband's work, but looking back I can see how I was doomed within the first couple months of working.

First, the pastor and church council were in panic mode and took their focus off of the life-changing gospel of Jesus, focusing instead on gimmicks and a "morality gospel." When I'm honest with myself, though, I recognize that I also took my eyes off of Jesus. I got caught up in the busyness of programming to increase attendance. As youth leaders, we must always remember that we can do nothing in our own strength. It is Jesus who gets us through the difficult times.

Second, being someone who is a "pleaser" by nature, I need to remember that God is my real boss. "Am I now trying to win the approval of human beings, or of God? Or am I trying to please people? If I were still trying to please people, I would not be a servant of Christ" (Galatians 1:10). Saying "no" to a new responsibility might upset someone, but God doesn't call us to do everything that others ask us to do. Saying "no" to a pastor is hard, and I did try it a few times, receiving negative

> God doesn't call us to do everything that others ask us to do.

feedback. I should have talked with my youth leadership team and asked for their help. They were my support system, and had I told them how stretched thin I was becoming, perhaps their voices would have helped. But ultimately, with or without their help, I only need to say yes to those things God is calling me to do, not what church leaders or parents expect of me.

Third, added responsibilities will naturally come with a job, and we need to be careful about those things to which we say "yes." When responsibilities change, communication is essential. When I first took on the elementary kids and subsequent new responsibilities, it would have been wise to document the decision as well as create a plan with the pastors to communicate my new responsibilities with the congregation and church leadership. As we continued to meet weekly, I should have taken notes on what we discussed, including action items done the past week and for the coming week and then emailed it back to her and my leadership team. It sounds like overkill, but such detailed communication would have been invaluable and would have made sure decisions couldn't be "forgotten." It would have created accountability, let leadership know what I was doing (avoiding the all-too-common *What does a youth leader really do all day anyway?* question), and kept us all on the same page.

Youth pastors go into ministry with a desire to help young people grow in faith by teaching, loving, and creating programs for them. I've never met someone who entered youth ministry because of a love of paperwork. But what I felt would have been micromanaging our meetings by taking minutes would not have been unspiritual. Rather, it would have been a disciplined way to make sure we were all on the same page. 2 Timothy 1:7 reminds us that "the Spirit God gave us does not make us timid, but gives us power, love and self-discipline."

Youth ministers can easily become overwhelmed with job responsibilities. Let's face it: We love what we do and are passionate about making a difference. And no job description we are given when we interview can ever really capture what we'll be doing. For example, "Build relationships with youth and their families"—everyone will have a different interpretation as to how the youth minister should go about it. And that could take two hours per week or 40 hours per week depending on the youth minister's personality.

Keeping our eyes on Jesus, pleasing only God as we use the talents we've been given, and creating disciplined communication with pastors, leaders, and families will help us not become overwhelmed with our responsibilities so we can excel at what we're passionate about—changing the lives of young people through faith in Jesus.

QUESTIONS TO CONSIDER

Is there anything I'm being asked to do in my ministry role that is distracting me from something God is calling me to do? If so, how am I going to deal with it?

What are the gaps in my communication with my pastor, lay leadership, parents, and other ministry stakeholders; and how can I fix them?

In what ways can I create measurable, achievable goals to clarify some of the vague language in the job description?

MY WAY OR THE HIGHWAY

CONFLICT RESOLUTION AT ITS BEST AND WORST

Dan Lambert is Professor of Youth Ministry and Dean of the Degree Completion Program at John Brown University in Siloam Springs, Arkansas, where he has served since 2000. He has been involved in youth ministry since 1982 and is the author of *Teaching That Makes A Difference*.

"The elders expect you to be in your office at church 8 a.m. to 5 p.m., Tuesday through Friday, and 8 a.m. to noon Saturday. You have Monday off and half a day Saturday. Any time you spend with the youth is on your own time. We pay you to be here, not playing with kids."

Those shocking words came from my senior pastor just a few weeks into my first job as a youth pastor at a local church in the Indiana countryside. During my previous four years at Youth for Christ, I went to plays, concerts, ball games, practices, kids' houses—my ministry was 80% being with kids. This church knew that. They supported my YFC ministry. Most of their youth group members were active in my club. That's why they came to me and asked me to become their youth pastor.

What happened? How did I get here? What should I do? All those questions and many more echoed through my mind.

> "We pay you to be here, not playing with kids."

I started my ministry at the church just as I said I would: by getting to know the young people and their parents. I visited homes, went to schools, learned family connections, listened to stories, and hung out doing whatever the kids wanted to do. Apparently, that's what started the problem.

One of the kids, a junior named Tony, wanted to go play a round of golf. I had a set of clubs and liked to hack around, so we went one August afternoon. We had a great time. I learned a lot about him and his passions; then we went to get a shake afterwards. All in all, it was a great few hours of ministry.

As it happened, one of the elders was driving by and saw us on the third hole green. He called the pastor after he got home that night.

"What was Dan doing out golfing with one of the youth in the middle of the day?"

The senior pastor tried to defend me. "He's getting to know the youth, just like he said. He *is* the youth pastor."

"What if there was an emergency? What if someone needed him for something else?" the elder continued. (Those seem like odd questions now, in a day where we all have cell phones at the ready.)

The elder persisted and called the other elders. It seemed they agreed with him, so they directed the pastor to communicate their dictum to me the next morning.

> **It all started with a set of bad assumptions.**

It all started with a set of bad assumptions. First and foremost, I was the church's first youth pastor, and they didn't have a job description. They agreed that we would work together on that during my first year, as the job developed. I thought it sounded like a great idea at the time. I assumed that I would do youth ministry at this church just as I had done it with YFC. The elders assumed I would be in my office all the time.

By the way, they also told me that if I went to youth camp as a counselor, I had to use a week of vacation. I only *had* one week of vacation.

So, I had a series of decisions to make. I had to decide what I would do with my new restrictions. I could give up, get mad, and quit. After all, how can a youth pastor do youth ministry tethered to his office all day long? Especially since this was before the Internet or cell phones that could have aided communication under the circumstances.

My wife and I decided not to give up quite yet. Enough parents were in my corner to make it worth the risk to stick around. My next decision concerned how to do youth ministry during my "off hours." Again, my wife and I discussed options. We didn't have children yet, so that helped. She was very interested in my ministry and wanted to be with me as often as possible—another plus. We didn't have any other obligations that would keep me from evenings and weekends with the youth. We would just have to sacrifice my hours and days off to make it work for a while.

My hope was that maybe over time I could win the elders over to my way of doing youth ministry.

I started by planning "Brown Bag Lunches" so kids could come to my office during the day and hang out. I organized an activity designed to get me into the homes of the youth; I called it "Chores With Dan." In a rural farming community, that led to some pretty interesting encounters with chickens, pigs, horses, goats, etc.

After school started, I dedicated my days to reading and planning excellent lessons. I spoke with every visitor who darkened the doors of the church building. I spent extra time with the pastor, just talking. In the evenings and on the weekends, I was at the schools for any event that was on the calendar, usually with my wife at my side.

As a result, we saw the youth ministry grow both spiritually and numerically. We had a good team of volunteers and some excellent leadership among the teenagers. I fulfilled other duties as well, when the senior pastor was gone. Hospital visits became one of my favorite things to do. They got me out of my office, and I got to meet some new people.

Since this strategy seemed to be working, I kept this up for a couple years. One day, out of nowhere, the pastor called me into his office again.

"Dan, remember when the elders told you that you were paid to be in your office and not out goofing off with the youth? Well, they met last night and that came up again. They are impressed with the work you've done and the growth in the group. They realize they were wrong and want me to let you know that you are no longer bound to office hours."

I was stunned and thrilled all at the same time. I expressed my appreciation and gratitude. But he wasn't done.

"They also want you to go to youth camp and take them on retreats and to concerts without sacrificing days off or vacation time."

It was better than Christmas for me. I had been hoping to hear words like that, but I honestly never thought I would. I spent five more great years there before accepting a call to another ministry. I have told this story many times in classes and workshops, so I have had a lot of time to reflect on the dynamics involved. While I am very humbled by what God did in and through me over those years, my decision to obey the elders without fighting went against every grain of my personality at the time. I was typically argumentative and anti-authoritarian. I can only credit the Holy Spirit for stifling my natural urges at the time.

I knew that I was serving under the authority of the elders and needed to submit to their will or resign. That biblical imperative is what guided me, even though my flesh wanted to fight. I also kicked myself a thousand times for taking a job without a job description. I was taught better than that by my professors and mentors, and my gut told me it was a bad idea. My ego, however, convinced me that I was different and that I could make it work.

When I shared this with others, after the initial indignation wore off ("How can a church expect a youth pastor to do youth ministry without 'spending time with youth' being part of his job?!"), the lessons became easy to discern:

1. Always have a clear job description *before* accepting a new job. Always.

2. When in doubt, it's best to submit to the will of the elders, even when it seems counterintuitive. (The obvious exception to this is when they are vio-

lating biblical teaching. In my case they weren't; they were simply disagreeing with my ministry philosophy.)

3. Adversity can breed creativity when we let it. Rather than throwing up our hands and giving up, we can get someone to help us think through our options, like my wife did with me in this case. Often the alternative plan will turn out to be better than the original.

> **Adversity can breed creativity when we let it.**

Many of those elders are still dear friends of mine, and after almost 25 years we still laugh about this story. I wish I could say that I have handled every disagreement with my supervisors in other ministries as gracefully as I did this one, or that all those disagreements turned out well. The truth that I only handled this situation well because I submitted both to the elders and to the Holy Spirit's counsel. Go figure.

QUESTIONS TO CONSIDER

What conflicts do I currently have with those in positions of authority over me? In what ways can I submit more, even if I disagree with their decisions?

What conflicts do I currently have with those of whom I am in a position of authority? In what ways can I become less autocratic and more of a servant-leader?

What are the predominant conflicts in my life right now? How can I reframe the conflict to find a creative, new solution that no one has considered yet?

WITCH HUNT
PARENTS' UNENDING LISTS OF WRONGS

Sally Chambers has been practicing youth ministry as part of her life with God and people for 20 years. By trade, she is a counselor, spiritual director, and aunty extraordinaire, as well. She lives in Nashville, Tennessee, where she is on staff with Saint Bartholomew's Episcopal Church. She is co-author of the leader's guide to *The Way of Pilgrimage* and the creator of "The Pilgrim's Way," an approach to leading pilgrimage with teenagers and adults through formative, monastic, and creative means.

You don't do it the way it's always been done.

You don't do it the way other churches do it.
You're stealing the teenagers away from everyone else.
Our teenagers don't come to services anymore.
You're not a team player.
You're resistant to authority.
You're a liability to the church.
And you're not churchy enough.

After 12 years of ministry, these things were communicated to me via letter from my rector prior to his departure on sabbatical. Come to find out several months later, several people were feeding this fire and vehemently seeking my termination. As more was unearthed, I discovered that much had been said behind closed doors and through email by our elected vestry.

Some of it had to do with issues that I thought had long been addressed and laid to rest. Some of it had to do with a summer of youth ministry trips and schedule conflicts. Some of it was true: our teenagers were bored and no longer participating in worship services with their families. Some of it was based on an "HR" interview that was very strenuous and almost staged. Some of it was an issue of differing theology and older practices of ministry. But all this to say, after 12 years of full time service, I had become the "problem" on the staff and in the church.

DILEMMAS

Context

What was particularly frustrating was that, as with most "witch hunts," the list of grievances had been lifted out of context in order to build a case against me. Context is essential to understanding and assessment. Context here included a staff that hadn't changed in six years, a rector who had been there more than 20 years, and me having served for more than 12 years. Why all the issues now? Why had no one come and asked me about any of these issues? Why were people so willing to accept them as truth? Why was I not trusted any more? The contextual questions seem endless.

Underhanded

In addition, no one ever sat down and directly asked me questions about context or clarification. The discussions were done behind closed doors and under the table. The first I heard of anyone being upset or having issues was the letter from my rector. And at that point it was a reprimand, not a conversation. I was shocked because I thought biblical conflict resolution would be normative in churches. When one person has an issue with another, he is to go directly to that person. If that doesn't work, he should take one or two others with him. Only then is it appropriate to involve the whole fellowship. Yet here I sat with a letter and reprimand without any effort to understand, clarify, or converse about the accusations.

Picking

Over the years I have learned that when people start "picking" at what and how a person does things, usually there is something larger at play. The "picks" are the excuse to some end. I was in such shock over being reprimanded in this letter; however, that it took me several months to clue in that a trap was being laid to force my termination while the rector was on sabbatical.

Accusations

Accusations are rarely helpful in the context of community and ministry. The Scriptures describe one being in particular as the Accuser, which makes me quite sure this is something I don't want to emulate. As hard as it sounds and as often as we all may be guilty of it, accusations leave little room for relationship, communication, questions, or love. Also, the accused is placed in a posture of self-defense, which is not helpful in efforts to work through conflict. In this case, I had a letter with accusations and very little means with which to defend myself. At that time, I didn't even know the names or faces of my accusers.

The Lone Wolf

As I processed what was contained in this letter, I began to ask the question, among others: how am I the only one responsible for whether our teenagers attend services with their families? I began to realize that I was left standing alone in things that were not (and should not have been) my sole responsibility. I had been allowed to work and minister for 12 years with very little but positive regard, at least outwardly. Now, I was becoming the scapegoat for an entire family of problems and issues.

The Scapegoat

Whether we like it or not, churches really are like families. New Testament scholar N.T. Wright, in *Acts For Everybody, Part I* (page 43), says that part of God's plan of salvation was to create a "new family" among followers of Jesus. Beauty and ugliness, joys and tears, kindness and cruelty, encouragement and gossip, health and sickness, passive mice and control freaks, busy bees and pew potatoes—they are all part of the mysterious family of faith called "the church." What this means, though, is that, just like in a family, problems are most often systemic, not just rooted in one person. But all too often one person gets labeled the scapegoat for a system that is no longer working.

Just like the old Hebrew practice of atonement where the scapegoat is sent off into the wilderness "carrying the sins" of the community, one person is blamed and "sent off" for the sins (systemic problems) of the community. The dilemma here is that obviously it's easier to get rid of one person than change a whole system. But the problem is that the un-health or dysfunction in the community continues after the scapegoat is long gone.

I remember clearly the moment it dawned on me, several months after this letter, sitting with the church leadership in the pastor's office, that I was playing the same role here at the church as I did in my alcoholic family growing up. How had I ended up here again? And this meeting had little to do with me, but was actually about handling one of the original accusers, one who had since become a lose canon.

> I remember clearly the moment it dawned on me that I was playing the same role here at the church as I did in my alcoholic family growing up.

Conflict

The hardest part lay in the decision: fight or flight? Do I stand up for myself, owning what I needed to own and rejecting the rest? Or do I sit down and receive the slap on the hand in the name of peace? Do I face conflict head on and work for change (within myself and within the system), or do I walk away and quit? Do I bury my head in the sand, hide in my office, and not disrupt the status quo? Do I turn the other cheek, or do I pick up a sword?

But let's not forget the hardest part of the hardest part: I have no control over what others will choose to do with this conflict.

Shame

One last dilemma I want to mention is that of shame. It's still hard for me to admit, but I was shamed by the letter, by the meetings and arguments about me behind closed doors, and by the reprimand. Forget about the letter on church stationary; I felt like I had been branded with a scarlet letter. I'll never forget having to walk into the first post-letter church board meeting, my face the shade of a scarlet letter. I literally stood outside the door taking some deep breaths and repeating to myself: *Hold your head high, and walk with integrity.*

The thing is that the shame was completely my issue. Shame was my response to the given circumstances. Shame was my insecurity and self-doubt. This meant, if for no other reason, I had my own work to do in moving through this.

HOW I RESPONDED?

The first thing I did was walk through the letter bit by bit with my pastor, making sure I understood what was being said and responding as necessary. I engaged in a conversation surrounding the issues, conflict, and "witch hunt."

I then took all of it, including my tears, to my spiritual director and other "older and wiser" folks. Together we tried to sort through truth from fiction. What did I need to pay attention to, and what I did not? And how should I respond?

I chose to not walk away, and I chose to not pretend like it hadn't happened. I chose to face the conflict and the pain (internal and external) in the hope of resurrection—the life that comes through the pain of the cross.

Since I was not being given an audience with my "accusers" or the church board, I responded with a letter. In the letter, I again attempted to engage in conversation surrounding each of the items on the list, bringing context and explanation into the mix while inviting participation in further conversation to seek answers to systemic issues. I asked further questions in the hopes of being able to work through the conflict. I received no response. In fact nothing was ever mentioned of it again…to my face.

I made intentional choices to engage in direct communication with everybody I could and began practicing courage instead of fear in the face of everyday conflict with others. I began practicing specific breath prayers in an effort to slow my reactions and transform my responses to others (since I was still a little on the defense).

And I continued to ask others to not walk away, to not bury their heads in the sand, and to work through the systemic issues that had presented themselves.

WHAT WOULD I DO DIFFERENTLY?

I have thought long and hard about what I might have done differently. Truth is, I'm not sure it's clear what would have helped or what could have been different. The bottom line when it comes to conflict (and witch hunts are ultimately about a conflict that underlies everything on the list) is that both parties have to be willing to work through it. I chose to stay and try for healing and resurrection.

Ironically just over a year later, my pastor told me it was time for me to leave. So I no longer work there any more. Even after being branded as scapegoat and sent away, I still believe that choosing to stay and face the conflict in hope of redemption, resurrection, and healing was the best choice for the community and for myself. Having to face my own issues that led to shame was also a good and healing thing for me, and for any future ministry in which I will participate. And as painful as it was, accepting the limits and the choices of others was and is, a good and necessary thing.

QUESTIONS TO CONSIDER

Have I (whether intentionally or unintentionally) ever been a part of a "witch hunt" toward someone else? If so, what were some of my underlying motivations, and how could I have handled them differently? If not, can I imagine otherwise good, godly people participating in such a thing?

The fight or flight options may seem to be two extreme responses to this kind of scenario, but what are some nuances of staying to "fight" through the dysfunction that are important for a Christian minister? What are ways to leave ("flight") honorably and well?

Though we often feel witch hunts come out of the blue, most often tension has been brewing under the surface for quite some time. While we can never completely predict others' behaviors, what are some safeguards we can build into our atmospheres and structures that will provide multiple opportunities for issues to surface before they reach boiling point?

BUDGET CUTS
THE GOOD, THE BAD,
AND THE NECESSARY

Josh Bishop is the Student Ministries Pastor at Mars Hill Bible Church, in Grand Rapids, Michigan, where he's been serving in youth ministry for 10 years. He is also earning his master's degree in social work from Michigan State University, and you can follow him on Twitter @joshdbishop.

When I became the student ministries pastor, I inherited a team of 11 staff members. Less than ten months later, only six of us were left—not because of power struggles or moral failings, but simply because of budget cuts.

I knew that the budget was not looking good, and I assumed that I might have to cut back a little. But national economic instability mixed with some local factors caused me to realize it wasn't going to be as simple as a few dollars here and there.

My supervisor brought me into a room and pulled a complicated spreadsheet out of a folder. It had every position of our staff listed with a lot of different numbers and formulas. I did not need to understand the details of the spreadsheet to know what it meant. My heart sank as I realized I was looking at a drastic restructure of our staff. My mind drifted from my supervisor's words, and I found the column labeled "Student Ministry Team." I knew I was going to have to fill in the positions that would remain and the positions that would be eliminated. I instantly saw the faces of all the good, hardworking, talented people who were going to lose their jobs. In that moment, the reality of the situation was too shocking to fully grasp.

For weeks, we worked to figure out the best way to keep our church moving forward and functioning in the failing economy. Eventually, the only way to find some balance was for me to restructure my staff, eliminate some positions and let some amazing staff members and friends go. The most terrifying day was the day I had to look several people in the eye and tell them that although they had done nothing but work hard, make personal sacrifices, and do a fantastic job, they were about to be among the millions of unemployed Americans. These were friends. These were people I had mentored. I had told them how much I believed in them and how bright their futures were. I had committed to helping them grow into their full potential. Now, I was telling them how many days they had left to work.

It was one the most difficult things I have ever had to do in my life. As the dust settled, I looked towards a future that appeared to require my team to do all the same work, but with about half the amount of team members.

The silver lining is that this difficult situation taught me some really important lessons.

THE DILEMMAS

A budget cut—whether it includes staff eliminations or simply a shrinking program budget—is a loss. Whether it's programs, ministries, or jobs that are the casualties of a budget cut, something is being tragically lost. During the budget crisis I faced, I learned that any experience of loss requires a few very important activities in order to maintain health.

First, I had to name the loss as a loss. Yes, it's just work; and, yes, no one died; but it is still a tragic loss. In order to move on from denial—a dangerous coping mechanism that prohibits emotional recovery—to some sort of recovery, I had to look myself in the mirror and admit it was a tragic loss.

Second, I had to allow myself to grieve. Pain and sadness are not emotions that we like to feel. In addition to that reality, we often live under the unspoken expectation that we are supposed to be happy all the time in ministry. This, of course, is an extremely unhealthy way of living, far from realistic, and a danger to our humanity. This is the lifestyle that leads so many in ministry to burnout, and to an inability to minister to others. Allowing myself to grieve was not only good for me, but it gave others the permission they needed to feel sadness along with me, which was the final step I needed—grieving with others.

I knew that the minute I believed I had to carry the tragedy of the situation alone was the minute I began to deteriorate as a leader and as a person. I needed to talk about my losses, and allow others to help me to feel and understand my emotions. I knew that if I did not work through the pain associated with my losses, they would become a lens through which I saw and understood myself, and my ministry. I had seen unresolved pain lead to bitterness, anger, cynicism, and depression; and I had seen good ministers' abilities to help others quickly fade. Looking back, I only wish I had realized that going through these dramatic budget cuts and losses was a really good reason to schedule an appointment with my counselor.

MY RESPONSE

Navigating budget cuts required an intentional focus on my personal health, but it also required an intentional focus on the health of my ministry. It was a true test of the strength and resilience of my ministry. When finances and resources were stable, decision-making filters were loose, and it was easy to expand in several different directions. It was simple to say yes to a new idea, when adding that new idea would not come at the expense of something else. In fact, new ideas often brought life and energy.

During tighter budget times, things were different. Conservative budgets forced me to make decisions between two good alternatives. In that reality, new ideas became a source of stress, and I had to learn to ask, "If I add this new idea, what will I have to drop in order to keep my ministry sustainable?" But during dramatic budget cuts, the situation got even worse. There was no room for new ideas; in fact, I was solely concerned with how to manage the current programming.

Thankfully, I had a centralizing force to act as a filter for what was essential and what was not. I knew that having a vision or direction for a ministry was important, but I also knew that a vision was not a specific enough standard to adequately help make difficult decisions. The most important factor for successfully navigating my budget crisis was being aware of a distinct calling for the ministry I led.

A calling is not just some mystical experience where one hears God's voice or a vision from a dream. A calling is an intersection of a couple very important elements. The first element is a fundamental awareness of a community's greatest needs. This goes beyond knowing the demands or desires of the community. It is not just what students or parents are asking or hoping for, and it is not simply what we think or assume they need. It is a deeper awareness of where the community is and where it is going, as well as who the community is and who it is becoming. The second factor is a brutal honesty about a ministry's strengths and resources. A community may need something specific—but if the necessary resources or the required skills to serve that need do not exist, the ministry needs a leader with the maturity to confidently and openly point it in a different direction.

Thankfully, in the year before our budget cuts, I had spent a lot of energy and hard work seeking to understand the intersection of my community's needs and our ministry's greatest strengths and resources. For me, the budget cuts sharpened what I considered one of the most important roles I have as a youth pastor, which is to absolutely know and be able to articulate the fundamental and unique calling we have in the lives of our students. An infinite amount of good ministry ideas exist, but the leader's role is to decide which ones will be pursued. I had been taught earlier that I simply could not implement every good idea that came my way.

I had also been convinced that God is doing all kinds of amazing things in my students' lives, and that I should not buy into the lie that my ministry was their only hope. I had spent a year answering the question, "What are we called to do in the lives of students?" And nothing helped me more during the budget crisis than knowing exactly what the answer to that question was. If you don't know that answer to that question in your context, a budget crisis will force you to figure it out.

My advice? Don't wait for a budget cut; find the answer now!

IN RETROSPECT

Even though I absolutely did not want to experience these budget cuts, I knew they would force me to change. The question was whether I was going to, change for the good or for the worse. I wanted to avoid the instant cynicism, hopelessness, entitlement, and loss of passion I had seen others experience in similar situations. Instead, I hoped that this terrible situation would somehow cause personal and ministry maturation. I hoped it would bring people together and make my ministry stronger, more focused, and more effective.

Many have noted that we become like the things we worship. Budget cuts have a mysterious way of luring our attention (and worship) towards money. Ironically, the perception of having money taken away from us drives us to believe that we are more and more dependent on it. If we are not diligent, we begin to elevate money from its rightful place as a resource to an object of our affection. Money can become the elusive god that could rescue us from our woes if we could just find a way to get more of it.

Budget cuts offer us an opportunity to more fully understand Jesus' warnings about the love of money and our inability to worship both God and money. His warnings are not

> Budget cuts have a mysterious way of luring our attention (and worship) towards money.

> Money can become the elusive god that could rescue us from our woes if we could just find a way to get more of it.

> If we are not diligent, we begin to elevate money from its rightful place as a resource to an object of our affection.

simply ethical or theological; they are also ontological. If we allow money to define reality—as it so often can when we are faced with managing a shrinking budget—our very identity gets twisted. We move away from understanding ourselves as being made in the image of God, and we start to define our value in terms of dollars and cents.

> We move away from understanding ourselves as being made in the image of God, and we start to define our value in terms of dollars and cents.

Almost nothing was more effective than a budget crisis for helping me to see the necessity of finding identity in something larger than myself—something more valuable than money and more important than my work. If you have found yourself in the midst of a budget crisis, my prayer for you is that you will have the courage to lift your eyes beyond the horrifying role of budget-cutter to find a greater meaning and identity in the One whose love for you surpasses all line-items, expenses, and salaries—and who is with you through every tear, every difficult conversation, every blank stare at a spreadsheet, and every moment of grief.

May God give you discernment, wisdom, and peace.

QUESTIONS TO CONSIDER

If my budget were cut by 75% tomorrow, what choices would I make regarding the allocation of the remaining resources? 50%? 25%? 10%?

Are any of our current expenditures unnecessary? How could a laser focus on our unique calling help avoid some superfluous spending?

In what ways are my ministry budget and my personal/family budget similar? Where am I overspending? In what is my anxiety rooted?

APOLOGIES NECESSARY
WHEN WE'RE THE ONES WHO SCREW IT UP

Jay Delp is a former 13-year youth pastor veteran and "video guy," who combines ministry and media in a variety of ways coast to coast, from his Philadelphia-area-based campsite, and runs his own video production company called (shockingly) Jay Delp Productions. For the rest of the story, check out jaydelp.com.

It all started innocently enough. A dozen or so teenagers, two guides from the organization responsible for providing the canoes, and I were all heading to an unfamiliar (there's your first clue) southeastern Pennsylvania tributary for a two-day, one-night canoe trip. What better way to experience the great outdoors, stimulate group building, and stretch ourselves a bit physically and spiritually than to paddle, splash, swim, and float our way down a gorgeous Pennsylvania river, set up camp, cook supper over an open fire, get some well-deserved sleep under the stars, and finish the second leg of our journey before heading back to reality?

Spirits were high as canoes were unloaded from their trailers, loaded with cargo, and launched into the water along with their two-person crews. Manny and Brad, two top-notch young men with built-in rowdy streaks, were already rowing in circles providing some friendly off-shore taunts coupled with near-miss paddle splashes towards a few of our slower-to-get-their-vessels-launched duos.

It was a beautiful summer day, we were on time (as if that mattered...on time for what?), things were going smoothly, and I was with some of the finest young folks on the planet. The water seemed a bit shallower than expected, but I wasn't concerned.

I should have been.

And so our randomly-spaced flotilla of canoes meandered gently down the stream, merrily, merrily, merrily, (scrape) merrily, life is but a (scrape) dream. (Scrape, scrape.)

Multiple, loud, and obnoxious scrapes emanated from every canoe as they all came to a grinding and sickening halt. We hadn't even paddled half a mile, and all need for paddling had ended. Oh well, we just hit a short stretch of "low tide," so we'll just jump out of our canoes and pull our crafts downstream a bit and hop right back in for the rest of this floating adventure, right?

213

214 IT HAPPENS

Wrong. Honestly, I don't know if there was any "hopping back in" for the next eight hours! Here we were, just starting a two-day canoe trip in a river… no, creek bed…that didn't contain enough water to float a freshman on an inner tube let alone two semi-adult-sized passengers along with their tents, tarps, testaments, and Twinkies. Not good. We pushed and pulled our canoes one mile (scrape, scrape). Then, two (scrape, scrape). Three. The scraping was relentless. The jovial wise cracks and laughter diminished with each passing hour as the reality of our seemingly never-ending struggle slowly crept over us.

> The jovial wise cracks and laughter diminished with each passing hour as the reality of our seemingly never-ending struggle slowly crept over us.

I think I can safely say that I am a generally upbeat kind of guy, but I was having a very difficult time keeping my own spirits up let alone try to keep up the spirits of some in our group who were obviously struggling with more than the metal burden tugging at their arms. (Scccrrrraaapppeee!) Sure, there was the occasional, and I mean *very* occasional, perhaps 50-yard stretch of water just deep enough to keep our vessels from scraping bottom, but the rest of the river (and our hope) were short-lived as our spirits and canoes hit rock bottom time and time again.

Faces were flush with fatigue. Arms, backs, and legs burned from the constant strain of walking and dragging canoes over countless rocks (scrape, scrape).

I was definitely in over my head, while only in water not much over my ankles.

DILEMMAS

These amazing young people were too strong, gracious, and mature to lash out at their lanky leader; though I could see it in some of their eyes despite their forced smiles. I could hear it in their silence and diminishing eye contact with me (scrape). Frustration. Fatigue. Anger. And I'm sure they saw the same in my eyes. For perhaps the first time as a youth pastor, I felt helpless to "save the day" with a quick quip, idea, plan B, or instant fix. There was simply no easy way out of this fiasco.

Our vehicles were parked miles downstream, and our campsite still several miles away. Our "guides" weren't much help. No apologies. Little sympathy, or empathy. (Ssscrape!) Or at least I couldn't see any through the fog of my own fatigue and emotions. In fact, one of them was alone in a kayak that had very little trouble floating much of the time, which only made attitudes worse.

We eventually stopped to eat supper at a potential camp much further upstream than anticipated, prepared and ate supper largely in that same, now epidemic, silence. We had a decision to make, and I had to help make it… soon. Do we set up our tents, camp out and somehow attempt to complete our two-day canoe trip or abandon the event now before dark and find a way to get our canoes up to the road and our vehicles to us?

MY RESPONSE

One final look into the eyes of these courageous but totally spent (physically and emotionally) young people, and the answer was clear: Abandon ship.

We faced a very steep, fairly long embankment up to the road; but summoning the little remaining strength within us required to coax those canoes up to the road (and freedom from this hell) was a small price to pay compared to the thought of a second day even remotely like the one through which we had just suffered. A couple of the guys walked, ran, and hitchhiked, returning with our vehicles and canoe trailer. We were saved.

Of course, today whenever several of us who were part of that colossal fiasco of an event are together and one of us mentions the "canoe drag," we all laugh—but it was not at all humorous at the time.

IN RETROSPECT

Can you and I always check out every river before the day of the event? Probably not. Could I have done a better job of researching the stretch of river our guides had selected? Most definitely. I'm also sure I could have been more real (honest) with our group that day about my own attitudinal struggles— Struggles with anger, not towards them, but towards our so-called guides, and towards myself for letting everyone in the group down and putting them in such a difficult situation.

Endless "what if…?"ing about my past "failures" (both in life and in youth ministry) is not a particularly favorite or helpful hobby of mine, but looking back and seeing God working in and through situations and people where I was clueless at the time is a wonderful hobby I wish to pursue more and more (the "looking back" part, not the "clueless" part).

> Looking back and seeing God working in and through situations and people where I was clueless at the time is a wonderful hobby.

And therein lies the "rub" of life and ministry, doesn't it? Trusting that God is at work even if…okay, *when* (which is almost always) I am oblivious to God's working in my life and the lives of those to whom I am called to minister. If my ministry with students is all about me, then when things go horribly wrong I'll see it as a reflection on me as a person and my leadership (or lack thereof). My failure. My need to somehow save the day. My ego at stake.

We all recognize the fallacy of such thinking here in black and white, but it's not so obvious in the heat of youth ministry struggles, challenges, and failures. It's one thing to demonstrate the fruit of the Spirit when my youth group activity or event goes as planned or even better than planned, but it's quite another to demonstrate it while dragging a metal canoe down a shallow river bed along with several other "sufferers" who I helped convince to be there.

Sure, I could spiritualize this shipwreck of an event by proclaiming, "All my students stepped out of the boat and actually walked on water." But all of us called to the insane privilege of working with students must not wallow in the quagmire of our so-called "failures", but instead determine to live life leaning forward as Paul testified in Philippians 3:14 about his own "mark pressing." Or also like that in-your-face T-shirt message popularized after James Cameron's mega-hit movie *Titanic* that read, "The ship sank, get over it!"

I'm over them both—the Titanic that sank and the canoes that didn't (couldn't!).

Boat trips without water.

What a colossal canoe-sance.

(Scrape.)

QUESTIONS TO CONSIDER

In what ways can I be better prepared for events, especially special events that involve leaving the church property and/or staying overnight? How much backup planning is necessary in order to avoid some of the primary pitfalls that may occur?

When things don't go the way I'd like them to—especially when morale is low—what sorts of things should be front and center in my attitude?

What is my normal modus operandi during challenging times, and how can I transform that for the better?

MARRIED WITH CHILDREN
WHEN CHILDBEARING AND JOB SEEKING COLLIDE

Kenda Dean is a United Methodist pastor and Professor of Youth, Church and Culture at Princeton Theological Seminary. Her books include *The Theological Turn in Youth Ministry*; *Youth, Religion, and Globalization*; *Almost Christian*; *Practicing Passion*; and *The Godbearing Life*. Learn more at kendadean.com.

I interviewed for my first position as a full-time pastor when I was three months pregnant. On the way to the interview (which was 20 minutes from my apartment), I pulled over to the side of the road twice so I could throw up. I pulled over a third time to get gas, which sprayed all over me due to a pump malfunction. I was not having fun.

I hoped I looked serene when I walked into the parlor of University United Methodist Church, but my face was gray and I reeked of 87 octane unleaded. I settled into an armchair conveniently located near an exit (just in case). I gazed around the room, my head swimming, and took in the hopeful anticipation exuded by committee members whose expectant faces told me they sure hoped this would be their last interview.

I hoped so too.

To save you the suspense, I got the job, and spent several happy years serving University Church as their Associate Pastor for Youth and Campus Ministry. I was blessed with the supreme gift of a relaxed senior pastor who was secure enough in his own skin to let me make my own mistakes without taking them on himself (harder than it sounds, because I made some doozies). Tom's ability to treat me as a young colleague instead of as junior support staff afforded me tremendous freedom, and under his guidance and example, my pastoral confidence grew like an amaryllis plant after Christmas.

Yet my interview that April evening surfaced three dilemmas that present themselves to a lot of women when we negotiate our first jobs in ministry, including youth ministry.

DILEMMAS

Plenty of complex issues surround the job seeking process without throwing pregnancy in the midst, but three primary questions weighed on me as I approached the interview:

1. Should I tell them I'm pregnant?

Starting a job pregnant presents complications for the woman and her employer. In my case, I knew that the start date of the job (July 1) would put me at six months pregnant. I was due in mid-October—exactly a month into the new school year and only three months on the job. In other words, I would work with students for about four weeks, and then vanish to have a baby.

2. How much maternity leave should I ask for?

On one hand, I wanted to be faithful to my new position. The young people and their families at this church desired a youth minister who would not only chart the course of the ministry but also be present in their lives—and as for the campus ministry part of the job, I was starting that from scratch. How could I do that if I were to take an extended maternity leave, especially so quickly into a new position?

> I had seen pastors sacrifice their families on the altar of ministry; this not only destroys families, but ministries as well.

On the other hand, I knew time with a newborn was time you don't get back, and I wanted a chunk of time to adjust to being a new mom during our son's first few weeks of life. That was an extremely high priority in my life—even higher than serving this congregation. I had seen pastors sacrifice their families on the altar of ministry, and had no interest in going there; I'm convinced that this not only destroys families, but ministries as well.

3. How could I possibly fulfill my call as a youth minister and simultaneously live into my call as a wife and mother?

The job description for University Church's Associate Pastor for Youth and Campus Ministry was clearly written with Jesus in mind. The 12 disciples together could not have met the expectations outlined in that job description, which included about 16 bullet points (no kidding) ranging from worship leadership to the campus ministry initiative I mentioned earlier.

> The twelve disciples together could not have met the expectations outlined in that job description.

I did not see any way that one human being could meet the expectations of that job description—especially a human being who was in the process of learning how to be a parent. Of course the temptation is to tell the church whatever they want to hear: that we can do anything and everything, well and with style. And I wanted the job; how could I risk being less than what they had hoped for?

MY RESPONSE

1. Should I tell them I'm pregnant?

Quick answer: yes. For one thing, this was an integrity issue for me; I have always laid my cards on the table, which has won the respect of employers far more often than not (in fact, I can't think of a single time it has backfired). Then there was the practical concern: I couldn't keep being pregnant a secret anyway, especially if I began throwing up during the interview. Finally, there was the matter of context: if I had to withhold the truth to get a job, I knew this was not a place where I wanted to work.

This turned out to be a simple answer for me, but I still had to face the second dilemma.

2. How much maternity leave should I ask for?

My friend Drema gave me the answer: as much as I could get. Drema had two children while serving in parish ministry, so her advice was based on personal experience. "Ask for three months, full time, paid maternity leave," she told me. "You can always go back to work early. But once you have the baby, you don't want to wish you had more time and not have it."

This was the hardest part of the interview, because after I told them I was pregnant, the committee asked me directly what my expectations were for maternity leave. The church had never had a pregnant pastor before; this was uncharted territory for everybody. I gave the committee Drema's criteria: three months maternity leave, full time, paid. "I realize that I will have to convince you that I can do in nine months what it takes some people 12 months to accomplish," I told the committee. I had tipped off my references that this would likely be a question they would receive so that they could be prepared for it when the committee called them. The church was convinced; they granted the leave without question. It was the wisest negotiation I have made in any job I have ever had, anywhere—and it told me a lot about the way this particular congregation valued parenting.

But there was still the third dilemma:

3. How could I possibly fulfill my call as a youth minister and simultaneously live into my call as a wife and mother?

No quick answer here. If anyone else gets this worked out, please let me know. I had plenty of advice from colleagues on how to balance personal and professional time in ministry (and I listened to all of them, so I had lots of strategies to choose from). But I took one measure that helped enormously, and I have used it in every ministry position I have held since then. I prioritized the tasks in my job description with the personnel committee.

Even in the nauseous haze of my interview, I knew that agreeing to the job description the church had posted was unmanageable. I knew I could mount a pretty convincing case that I *could* do the things it listed; I had skills in all the task areas and a lot of energy to boot (as did everyone else they interviewed). But to promise to do the job as listed was both dishonest and irresponsible—and a fast ticket to disappointing the congregation and infuriating my spouse. Yet I *did* want that job. University Church had a growing congregation with a strong sense of mission to young people in the community. I had a good vibe on the senior pastor (the crucial ingredient for professional happiness), and it was in a location that allowed my husband to continue his doctoral work at the University of Maryland. You don't get opportunities like that every day, so I didn't want to squander it. So, impossible job description or no, when the bishop offered me the position, I took it.

But I did two things for sheer self-protection. First, during the interview itself, I asked the committee about its priorities for their Associate Pastor. I listened hard. I wanted to hear the way the personnel committee understood the job description—and what they sensed were the most important tasks of the ones listed. This committee ultimately would have to represent me in the congregation, and I would need their support if some tasks didn't get done. If their sense of priorities did not match mine, I knew I would not be a good fit for the position.

Second, once I accepted the position, I rearranged the tasks in the job description according to the priorities I had heard voiced by the personnel committee. Now the job description listed the top priority as #1, the next priority #2, and so on. When I wanted to rearrange the committee's priorities around, I did, but I picked my battles; I could defend shifting a couple priorities, but not all of them, so I picked the priorities that mattered most to me and made sure they were towards the top of the list. When I finished, I took the whole list back to the personnel committee. "As I understand it," I told them, "this is the way you would like me to prioritize my time." I gave them copies of my newly-ordered job description. Where I had flipped priorities, I explained why. Then I said, "Can you tell me if I have understood this clearly? Is there any priority you want me to rearrange?"

That got a lively discussion going, which was illuminating on a lot of fronts, but it also elicited hearty support. Just to make sure we were all on the same page, I reviewed the priorities and said, "Okay, this means I'll spend this fall working on #1, #2, and #3. Then, when we meet in December, we'll assess how those are going, and if it looks like we're ready, we can add #4." Since this committee was also supposed to represent the pastor's needs to the congregation, I added: "And if you hear someone in our church wondering why a priority further down the list isn't getting much attention, you can tell them why."

Everyone readily agreed—and this became our practice every year. Each spring we established the priorities of my work for the following year, proposed through a combination of my listening to the congregation's wants and needs, and my own pastoral sense of where the congregation needed to go. I don't think we ever got past priorities #5 or #6—even though the job description still listed all 16 different tasks that I was theoretically responsible for. Presumably, had I stayed at the church long enough, we would have worked through the whole list...or, maybe not.

The point is, prioritizing the job description allowed me to focus my energy and let some things go for the time being. That made the job more manageable in a way that satisfied both the congregation and me. Because of the priority list, for instance, I let go of developing a Friday night college recreation program in my first year. It was #11 or #12 on the priority list, and Friday nights were the one night of the week my husband and I were home together with our son. By the second year, the recreation program was in place—but not because I was leading it. A couple of sophomore guys decided to organize rec night themselves. At first, I was guilt-ridden that I wasn't joining them, even though it was still a low priority goal (and honestly, rec night sounded like a lot more fun than changing diapers). But then one of the guys, in an off-handed way, told me: "You know, we'd love to have you join us on Friday nights. But I think it's cool that you'd rather be home with your family. I've never known anybody who would rather be home with their family."

IN RETROSPECT

I could not have asked for a better first pastoral experience. Tom, the senior pastor, was the kind of colleague we pray for: he cared about my *vocation*— the integration of multiple callings into a life lived with others before God. Tom encouraged me to capitalize on my strengths and not obsess over my weaknesses. The nine or 10 people on the personnel committee showered our family with grace and gently taught me how to be their pastor. They also taught me a great deal about how to be a "professional minister" and a wife and mother at the same time. Some things worked better than others. (The playpen in the office was a bust; all I wanted to do was play with my baby.) Scheduling some meetings at the parsonage on nights my husband was at work was generally helpful (except for the night I let Brendan cry himself to sleep during a trustee meeting; I should have saved child-rearing experiments for the off-nights.)

University Church was not a perfect church for a young wife and mother, either. We never did provide childcare during church meetings or programs, and my husband never fully escaped the feeling of being "the minister's wife." Still, University United Methodist Church loved us through our young adult years, filling our lives with dear friends, partners in ministry, and surrogate grandparents for our new little "P.K." It made me believe that, given a chance, congregations want to make possible a pastoral life for their leaders—and not just a pastoral job. We just have to show them how.

QUESTIONS TO CONSIDER

Do I trust God during the interview process to be completely honest about my needs and priorities, or am I willing to manipulate the conversation to try to land the job?

What do I do when my priorities or needs change once I'm in the job and they don't synch up with others' expectations of me?

What communication processes do I need to establish now in order to be on the same page with my boss and church leaders regarding my priorities?

SURPRISE!
YOU'RE FIRED
FINISHING THE RACE
AND ENDING WELL

Brent Parker is the Associate Pastor for Family Life at First Christian Church in Longview, Texas. In addition to his work at the church, he also serves as a Lead Consultant with Youth Ministry Architects. Brent, his wife, Kori, and their sons, Caedmon and Kai, enjoy spending days together anywhere that balls can be thrown, caught, hit, dribbled, or kicked. More about Brent at thiswayministries.org.

Staff meeting had come to a close, and after making my way to the youth office to collect some papers that I needed for a Graduation Sunday discussion with my new senior minister, I opened the door to the church library—where he suggested we meet—to find him, our board chair, and our personnel committee chair seated on one side of the table and an empty seat for me across from them. Though he was well prepared to discuss commencement plans with me, it became clear over the next hour that it was not our high school graduates' sendoff that my new boss had arranged for us to discuss. It was mine.

Each of the three men took a turn describing why, after six years of ministry, I was "being given the opportunity" to resign. They outlined the severance package that I would receive if I kept silent, not revealing the truth of my departure and causing a stir in the church. They helped edit my letter of resignation, including the details of how I was heading off to seminary and moving into the next chapter of my ministry.

While these men felt as if this "silent dismissal" was a gift to me and to the church, I was boiling over with feelings of anger, sadness, and betrayal. In the days, weeks, and months that followed, I entered into a period of deep mourning and began the painful process of taking a personal inventory. It was in the midst of each that I found myself inundated with the nagging questions that haunt most youth workers when we are confronted by the dissatisfaction of others:

"What is wrong with those people?"

"Don't they know what I mean to this church?"

"Have they thought about the ramifications of this decision?

"Where in the world did they get that idea from?"

"Who do they think they are?"

After the self-serving, egotistical, and prideful questions had been asked, I then began to question God's role in this situation. I began to call into ques-

227

> I moved into a theological tussle with God, wrestling with issues and queries that I had not ever encountered before.

tion my own gifts for ministry. I moved into a theological tussle with God, wrestling with issues and queries that I had not ever encountered before. It was within this wrestling match that I found out who I really was…and uncovered an aspect of which I had not before appreciated.

THE DILEMMAS

What are we to do when our bosses or church leaders deal a crushing blow? How can we take steps forward into an uncertain future, after our own dreams and plans have been stymied by another? And how are we to understand the will—and character—of God within such a complex and painful scenario? The way I answered these questions, along with the choices I made over the next several months, played a pivotal role in the future narrative God was waiting to reveal.

I had recently announced to the young people that I would not be leaving for at least another year; my wife had just signed a contract to teach for another year; I had not applied to a single seminary; and my house was not yet for sale. Nonetheless, I was being asked to announce my planned resignation and entry into the next chapter of my life. My being asked to keep the truth away from the church family that had raised me, loved me, and supported me in ministry for six years made the first steps into the journey very difficult. While I was not yet prepared to move on, I had to make a decision about how to move forward.

The choice seemed fairly clear: Go quietly or make a scene. I played out both scenarios over and over in my mind. I imagined myself going to all of the families in the church who had supported me over the years and telling them all about the meeting in the library, the lying, and the horrible future that was ahead for them because of these "power hungry" men. I pictured these families all bonding together, marching into the minister's office and demanding that I be reinstated. I even daydreamed about how the church would ask the new minister to leave, would reprimand the thoughtless actions of these two men, and would rally to bring back more honorable processes of handling church business.

Then in my quieter moments, after the swell of ego and pride had run its course, I would begin to feel deep sadness for the people in our church who had no idea what was going on, who did not deserve to get caught up in the "ugly side" of the church, and who would ultimately be damaged spiritually by the sort of antics I had dreamed up as the best way of vindicating myself. I began to use language of "taking the high road" in my own internal conversations. Even after the very generous offer of a close friend in the church to personally provide me the severance package that had been offered in exchange for my silence, I was unable to "go public" with the story.

MY RESPONSE

I decided to go quietly. My wife and I had private conversations with her parents (her mom was an elder) and with a couple of families who, we trusted, would allow the discussions to be kept in high confidentiality. Together with them we began to pray and plan about what would be next. The way God invited us into our future narrative, and the details of our journey which further clarified God's accompaniment, can only be described now as I look back over the almost seven years since that experience. And when I have shared a cursory re-telling of these events to other youth workers in the midst of their own trials and turmoil, my hope is that they might be able to trust in the bigger picture of a bigger God.

Honestly, I had been praying for a while that God would open whatever doors were necessary for me to enter so that I might best do the will of God. I had imagined that God would open those doors slowly away from me, allowing me to take in the scenery of an unfolding landscape. Well, the door opened! In waiter terms, I had walked into the kitchen as someone else was heading out the same door, and the tray filled with my own plans, pride, and preferences went flying onto the floor, making a huge mess. It took a little time to bend down and pick up the pieces of the collision. I had quite literally encountered a collision between my plans and God's plans.

While on the floor, I was forced to consider what God really desired from me. I had been trying to please God with my efforts as a husband, dad, and youth minister. I entered into each day with the resolve to be all that I could be for God and for the people around me. I had come to believe that God's opinion of me, that any value I had in God's eyes, was directly related to how much I did for God and how well I did it. Meanwhile, stunned and disoriented by the collision, I began to hear again the words of God from Matthew 3:17: "You are my beloved. With you I am well pleased."

Then came Psalm 46:10: "Be still and know that I am God."

The words of Micah 6:8 then joined the chorus: "God has shown all you people what is good. And what does the Lord require of you? To act justly and to love mercy and to walk humbly with your God." The Micah text began to speak to me in a new and fresh way.

Walk humbly. Walk humbly. The final proclamation of the prophet is to do two things that I had not done very well for a long time: walk and be humble. I had been running at my pace, with my flags flying, and had collided with the movement of God that was headed in a different direction. I was confidently running in pursuit of the great things I wanted to accomplish that would further declare my ability as a youth minister. God knew that until I hit the wall, I would not receive the gift that had been intended for me all along.

> Two things that I had not done very well for a long time: walk and be humble. I had been running at my pace, with my flags flying, and had collided with the movement of God that was headed in a different direction.

God was offering me the opportunity to trust that I was enough just as I was. That my role as the youth minister at that church did not define me. In fact, it was God who defined me. God was inviting me into a journey that involved a slower gait. And as we walked along, Jesus took me by the hand and guided my family into the bigger picture of God's will.

IN RETROSPECT

As the result of my resignation and the subsequent chapters of my life since, God has allowed me to receive the gift of a theological education, uncovered spiritual gifts of discernment and pastoral care, opened doors for me to write and consult, and led me into the very places where I can be used to celebrate and to reveal the Kingdom of God among the people of God. I am now thankful for those three men who set me free to be who God has intended for me to be.

Could I and would I have done some things differently if I had to go through the same experience again? Sure! I probably would have actively squashed the stories that were coming out about my firing rather than allowing them to linger. Though it felt good to know that the truth was escaping, the conflicts that erupted after my departure, resulting in a small exodus of many families with youth, could have been avoided. Yet, the way that God has moved within and among those families, and in the churches where they landed, gives further evidence that God's ways are better than our ways (Isaiah 55).

If nothing else, I learned in that situation and many that have followed that we really can trust God in all circumstances because "we know that in all things God works for the good of those who love him, who have been called according to his purpose" (Romans 8:28).

QUESTIONS TO CONSIDER

How much of who I am is defined by what I do?

In what ways am I running when I should walk?

In what ways am I not as humble as I need to be?

If I were to be fired tomorrow, how would I respond?

Because good youth ministry doesn't just happen

In today's world, good youth ministry requires more than just games and guitars.

Whether you're a **youth minister** who wants training or a **church** in need of a stronger youth ministry, the Center for Youth Ministry Training is here to help.

For youth to experience a life-changing faith, they need an intentional community of teens and adults where they have a personal encounter with God, are encouraged to understand God's purpose for their lives, and find home in the intersection of their story with God's bigger story.

For this kind of youth ministry to happen, both youth workers and churches need training.

The Center for Youth Ministry Training brings together **Partner Churches** and **youth ministers** to create life-changing youth ministries through our **Graduate Residency in Youth Ministry**.

Other Resources from CYMT:

Hollow Faith
by Stephen Ingram

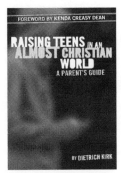

Raising Teens in an Almost Christian World
by Dietrich Kirk

For more information on the Center for Youth Ministry Training Graduate Residency program or to learn more about other CYMT resources visit www.cymt.org.

Made in the USA
Charleston, SC
08 November 2012